Winning Through Redundancy

Six steps to navigate your way to a brighter future

Steve Preston
The Career Catalyst®

Printed and bound in Great Britain by
CPI Group (UK) Ltd, Croydon, CR0 4YY

ISBN 978-1-907798-42-9

Dedications

This book is dedicated to:

Sue Blake - For your inspiration, wisdom and belief in me to become a published author of note. You are sadly missed but your light still shines on us.

Dad - For providing me with the inspiration to win through redundancy and dedicate my business in your honour. We all miss you dearly but I know you are smiling down on us and sharing my success.

Leanne and Paul - For making me such a proud dad. The world is your oyster. Keep following your passions and live your dreams!

PRAISE

About The Book

"Changing jobs for any reason can be the great turning point in your career and in your life. This book shows you how to make the rest of your work life the best of your work life."

Brian Tracy – Author, *Earn What You're Really Worth*

"Redundancy! Just the very word fills so many with fear, doubt and stress. Those worries can now be phrased in the past tense. With Steve Preston's excellent new book: Winning Through Redundancy - anyone can regain control of their lives, their results, and their future.

Dive into the Cycle Model and discover just how much you have to offer. Take a fresh P.E.R.S.P.E.C.T.I.V.E. on everything in your life and realise that even an unseen redundancy is the first day of the rest of your life.

Steve's down to earth, clearly defined, practical ideas are just what anyone facing redundancy or who's recently experienced it is looking for. It's your guide to the future, a road map to new successes, and a friend always by your side. Read on - you'll be so pleased you did."

Peter Thomson - The UK's Most Prolific Information Product Creator

"I wish I had read this book ten years ago when I was questioning my career and my life. I love how Steve demystifies the process and emotions that people go through when making a career change and offers clear practical steps, help and guidance. **This is not just a book about redundancy, it is a book about how to take your life in your hands and follow your heart.** *Thank you Steve!"*

Tara W Cox

I'm wondering if you're saying to yourself "Not another one of those 'self-help' books" ...and you'd be right! ...it's NOT another one of those self-help books. This one takes quite a different slant and focuses the attention of those people who have become 'lost' following redundancy and need some help to get back on the right track. Therefore the issue isn't whether or not to read Winning Through Redundancy, it is whether you can afford not to, as Steve Preston's Career Navigation Cycle is a process that leads people from darkness to light... and I should know.

"It was my logical mindset that refused to neither understand nor accept why I was facing redundancy and I desperately needed guidance to help me through the darkness. Steve's 'Career Navigation Cycle' is a lifeline that sits at the core of his outplacement programme and book and this presented me with a rational, systematic process to follow. The topsy-turvy 'roller coaster' journey allowed me to 'let go' of the past and regain confidence whilst building a sense of realisation and liberation that I could pursue something I truly enjoyed and life became much brighter and exciting filled with possibilities. The easy style of the book reads as if you're having a chat with a friend who is keen to give advice and stimulus to move you forward to achieve your true potential. Steve's wealth of experience and passion will positively propel you, like me, to a new era that you may not have thought possible.

It's true isn't it, we all keep medicines in readiness to help recovery when we're unwell? In today's unstable economic environment it would be wise to keep a copy of Winning Through Redundancy in the First Aid Box as something Steve can prescribe for you ...you never know when you'll need it!"

Steve Engwell

"Steve's book is 'The Knowledge' of how to turn your career transition into a challenging yet positive and uplifting life changing experience. A must have guide for anyone embarking on a new voyage of career discovery!"

Gail Gibson

"This isn't the sort of book that most people will buy for a relaxing read, although you will be pleasantly surprised, as I was. It will be read by people, who like me, find themselves at the crossroads of their working life, mainly as a result of redundancy. **It will also appeal to people who want to change career because of a lack of fulfilment in what they are doing to earn a living.**

It is often a huge step to seek help and then once that step is taken, to find the right advice to help move you forward on a 'voyage of self discovery'. This book becomes your friend and your mentor as you take stock of your life and look at how you can reinvent yourself as you 'navigate your way to a brighter future'.

As you read through each step prescribed by Steve, you will soon feel relaxed as you realise that he is talking to you and you alone. The style of the writing makes you feel as though you are having a one on one session with Steve himself! At each stage of the book you are challenged to think about where you are in your life and where you want to be. It invites you to re-evaluate your priorities. It questions your thinking and makes you step outside your comfort zone. All this is done in a way that is not intrusive or threatening. It makes you feel good about what you need to do to change your career or job.

You have reached out your hand and asked for help and Steve has responded in a compassionate, caring way that makes you sit up and take notice and then actually take the next step towards 'becoming the architect of your own future'.

Having read the book, I am more relaxed about the next step in seeking employment or whatever I choose to do. Each day is a day further away from my previous employer and a day further away from the feelings that go with redundancy. I now know don't have to rush into getting a job but, as Steve says, I obviously don't want to spend all my redundancy pay and then suddenly wake up!"

Ewen Anderson

"At last a book that tackles redundancy in a positive, motivational and practical way, giving the reader the opportunity to handle their own situation with passion, energy and enthusiasm at a difficult time in their lives.

This book is crammed with information based on Steve's personal experience and many motivational and inspiring case histories. I particularly liked the fantastic practical exercises and common sense style that Steve uses to help you achieve what you really want at the next stage of your career.

The six steps are logical, chronological, easy to follow and will help you not only now but throughout your future career and life.

Highly recommended for people who are serious about success and fulfilling their true ambitions and dreams by finding their ideal job or career."

Don Presland

PRAISE

for Steve's Career Coaching Work

"Steve is expert in unlocking potential and helping clients make an impact. His coaching methods and materials are thought provoking, engaging and deliver results."

Dean Creamer, OBE

"I would describe Steve as the 'Anthony Robbins' of job seeking. This man takes any negative thinking and re-frames it as positive outlook. Put bluntly I was lucky enough to be on one of Steve's workshops and before I met him 'I couldn't get arrested'. Two weeks after his course I had over 3 job offers from stock brokerages. There should be more people in this country like Mr Preston and you can take that to the bank!!!!"

Liam Byrne

"Steve's knowledge and understanding of the science of work and career is exemplary. His ability to see how to help others to realign their internal belief systems with their need to work produces explosive results. This helps you to attain new goals and create new work pathways that had not previously been considered available or possible before. His Breakthrough Career Change Masterclass is

inspiring, creative and an essential rewiring for the brain of somebody at a dead end."

Simon Dwight

"Steve is one of the UK's market leaders in Career and Personal Development. He is incredibly skilled in unlocking and opening your mind to believing in and fulfilling your own true potential". Steve is in demand; work with him while you can!

Debbie Smith

"I engaged Steve's support during my transition to independence, following many years of working within the corporate environment. It was a key point in my life where I needed to stop and reflect upon what my future held. Steve along with his associates coached me through a number of key areas in order for me to confidently pursue my personal goal and the process of re-branding myself as 'ME'. The power of coaching is not fully understood until you have experienced it firsthand. With Steve's extensive knowledge and a never ending 'toolkit', it makes the process not only enjoyable but an empowering one that I can fully recommend."

Jane Seeley

"I've worked with Steve and the team at SMP Solutions for a number of years and cannot express enough how supportive they've been in helping with my personal career development over the years. Through their support I've transitioned from a manager of a technical support department at a college to running my own businesses and finally getting a good work-life balance. The advice, guidance and support has been (and still is) truly valuable as I continue to personally develop and as my company grows!"

Lee Dredge

"When I first met Steve, I was 'lost' and had no idea of what I wanted to do with my career and life. Steve gave me a sense of direction and took me on an empowering journey of exploration. I came to realise it was OK to be 'different' and 'me' and that I don't have to follow the typical job or career route. I came away with some comprehensive and powerful tools, which have now shaped my thinking about myself and the work I can and want to do. I highly recommended Steve as someone who is a great coach, genuinely cares and is passionate about making a difference to you and your life."

Dee Patel

"I was introduced to Steve at a time when I was considering my future career options. Steve brought a wealth of experience, tools and insight to help me understand myself better and how I could approach my career, job searches and interviews. Having recently gone through a redundancy process I called on Steve's services again and he was an integral part of my transitioning successfully to a new role."

Adam Thomas

"Working with Steve has made a real and lasting difference to my life - sounds dramatic but it's true. His way of working really resonated with me; we had fun but got through a whole load of difficult stuff! Steve helped me to find a good work-life balance, to recognise what I had to offer and to have the confidence to demonstrate it to others. As a result, I am more focused at work, achieving great results that others are recognising and happier at home. Steve has continued to be a confidante and friend to me and I am so pleased to have met him."

Lisa Hughes

"When I was stuck in a rut and looking to develop my career to the next stage, I enlisted Steve's help to provide the focus and clarity I needed to ensure that I was applying for the right jobs and to also market myself in the most effective way. Steve helped me to really understand my true marketability, what was important to me in my next role and motivated me to achieve job success. He is encouraging, professional and expert and I highly recommend him for any professionals and executives looking to develop their career."

Richard Castleton

Acknowledgements

I wish to thank many people who have helped turn my vision into reality to achieve my goal of becoming a published author of a book which will make a difference to the lives of others.

To my wonderful wife, Lin, for your love, patience, encouragement, unbending support and being my sounding board and rock throughout this emotional roller coaster labour of love.

Mum, for encouraging me to be independent, follow my dreams and always do what makes me happy.

Ed Peppitt, a font of knowledge and a wonderfully generous man whose publishing workshops inspired me to take the leap of faith and turn the book inside me into reality. Without you none of this would be possible.

Leda Sammarco, my Writer's Coach for sharing my vision, starting me on the journey and keeping me on track to secure a publishing deal. Your coaching and ongoing support has been invaluable.

Tara Winona, my amazing Illustrator, for bringing my book to life with your vision, passion, vibrancy, energy and incredible art. Isn't it fantastic the process has helped you find another passion to share your creative genius with the world!

Caroline Swain, my brilliant Copyeditor. A 'human Rottweiler' with grammar and words. You have changed my life forever now I understand the meaning of 'tautology'!

Don Presland, my lifelong best mate and beer buddy for your constant support and eagle eyed critique.

Debbie Smith, for your encouragement, belief and friendship, sharing in many successes and for kindly providing material on Personal Branding.

Gail Gibson, for your proofreading, inspiration, support, friendship, and input for Portfolio Careers, Networking and Social Media.

Steve 'Sherlock' Engwell, client now friend and associate for your all round brilliant support. I feel privileged to have supported you to win through your redundancy and helped bring out your latent creativity and natural talents to take you 'from the darkness and into the light'.

Steve Bridger for kindly providing information and inspiration for the self employed career options from your excellent 'Success Before Start-up' book and workshop.

Rob McCargow, Cadence Partners, London, for kindly introducing some wonderful clients and providing content for Interim Management.

Brian Tracy, a brilliant speaker, author and psychologist and a source of constant inspiration.

Peter Thomson, business guru and 'Product Creation genius'. Your workshops inspired me to stretch and create products that will make a difference to the lives and careers of others.

To all my clients and contacts who have agreed to be featured in the various case studies in real name or pseudonyms to protect your identities. You are testimony to what can be achieved with the right mindset, belief and positive actions.

Finally, to all my past, present and future clients who give me the ultimate reward of sharing in your successful career transitions to do work you love and lead fulfilling lives. I thank you all.

CONTENTS

INTRODUCTION

By reading this book you will transform your life following redundancy or if you are looking to change career. You will feel energized; develop a real sense of purpose and focus. People I work with tell me *'that the clouds will lift'* giving you clarity, self awareness and a target to aim for. You will be much better equipped to know what is important to you in your life and career moving forward, understand what you have to offer an employer or what you can offer as a business owner, to sell yourself effectively and above all know what it takes to make a successful career change or transition. Once you have developed this inner self awareness you will be in a good position to take the learning and knowledge you have gained into the world of work whatever you decide to do.

I will be sharing some of my journey following redundancy. Many of my learning points, as well as some interesting and inspiring case studies, will show you how you can win through redundancy to *navigate your way to a brighter future* and relaunch your career!

Each Chapter relates to a step of my Career Navigation Cycle and has specific exercises and tools which are all part of the process to help you achieve a successful outcome. My aim is to inspire you to get started on your journey and ultimately 'take the leap of faith' to find the right job, career or work for you. Isn't it reassuring to know that, you like me and many of the case studies featured, will also come to '*love Mondays*', enjoy the work you do and achieve a fulfilling life?

How Do You Feel About Your Career?

To put your first stake in the ground, consider the following statements and put Y (yes) or N (no) as applicable to you after each statement or on a separate document or piece of paper.

1. I see my redundancy as a threat and an uncertain future
2. I see my redundancy as an opportunity to re-evaluate my career
3. I don't know where my career is heading and feel totally lost
4. I've been in the same job or industry for years and feel stuck in a rut
5. I am concerned about my age in the current job market as employers want younger people
6. I am not achieving my full potential and was bored with my previous job
7. I would like to find work that is fulfilling but I'm afraid of trying something new
8. I want to make a career change but have so many ideas I can't decide what I should do
9. I want to progress my career but am having trouble getting interviews and becoming very disheartened
10. I am getting interviews but no job offers so feel like giving up
11. I would like to start my own business, but don't know whether I am capable of making it work or where to begin
12. I have been spending too much time working or commuting which has affected my health, family and social life
13. I dread applying for new jobs

I would hazard a guess that you have at least two Yes's, haven't you? Whatever your number, this book can help you re-evaluate what you want from a future job or career. If you are feeling unhappy or uncertain as a result of your redundancy, you are more than likely to have several Yes's, in which case you will definitely get real value from this book, so read on.

If you are feeling happy and optimistic about your redundancy, likewise this is great. As you read on I will help you stay positive and proactive whilst also discovering how to avoid some of the many pitfalls I made following my redundancy and have seen many other people make since. Regardless of how you currently feel about your career or redundancy, you can be assured that this book will help you navigate the career transition maze in a more focused and confident way, with a proven process to follow to achieve your desired outcomes. If you are unable to see this far ahead, don't worry as I will guide you through the process to help you create a new vision for your success.

My Story

In 2001, I found myself facing redundancy. Even though I had months to prepare myself and saw redundancy as an opportunity to make a clean break after twenty mostly enjoyable years with my company, I felt as though the rug was being pulled from under me and did not know what I wanted to do next. By the time I left, for the first time in my career, I had no real strategy or sense of purpose. I was lost!

If you are facing, or recently experienced redundancy, you too are at a career crossroads and likely to feel lost, anxious or simply uncertain about how to move forward. You may also lack confidence, motivation and self belief to make a successful career transition following redundancy.

Don't worry as these are natural responses and you are not alone. Although it may not seem like it to you, I can assure you that there are many other people in exactly your situation and you, unlike many others, at least have the benefit of reading and taking the learning from this book to put you ahead of the game.

Interestingly, research over the last decade consistently shows that 1 in 2 people is in the 'wrong job' and 2 out of 3 are unfulfilled in their jobs. Therefore millions of people who experience redundancy may well have been unhappy and in the 'wrong job' anyway, so redundancy can often be a blessing in disguise! However, when the rug is pulled from under you i.e. your redundancy is a bolt out of the blue, you are likely to experience completely different emotions than if you surprised your employer by choosing to leave of your own accord. When you are in control of your decisions and career it is much easier to be positive about the future, which is why it is often difficult for many people to view redundancy as an opportunity. Your initial reaction is likely to be negative because your employer has taken away your control and you might feel helpless. I will show you throughout the book how you can change your thinking so you learn how to take control of your career and life, not just now but for the rest of your working life.

In my case, I had already started exploring a few opportunities before the redundancy consultation started because I was beginning to feel stuck in a rut and unfulfilled. Although the announcement came as a shock, I saw redundancy as a real opportunity for me to start over and was initially very positive about my situation. However, once I had left the company and the initial sense of relief from 'severing the umbilical cord' wore off, the realisation kicked in that I had no idea what I wanted to do next, how to spend my time and that I faced an uncertain future! Maybe you recognise these feelings? If so, you have the reassurance of knowing that I will help you to relaunch your career and create the path to finding fulfilment in your work and life, just as I did over a decade ago.

Prior to redundancy I'd built a successful 30 year career in the travel industry working for a range of companies including household names such as Thomas Cook and British Airways. My last 20 years were spent in management in what started out as Pickfords Travel and ended up as Going Places, which is now ironically owned by Thomas Cook. I started as a Branch Manager then moved up the ladder into a variety of roles. My career progressed quickly in a typical linear fashion into Area Management and onto a spell as a Board Director. At the time of my redundancy, if I had recognised then what I know now, I had already been through many major career transitions as a result of the multitude of reorganisations, acquisitions, mergers and changes of ownership. I had to reapply for my job on a number of occasions and whilst I was always saved from the axe, it was an unsettling time which invariably left a bad taste. Unfortunately, you become so conditioned to such changes and upheaval that you start to take this as the norm in large organisations. This is a sad reflection on the world of work but, like me, most people hang on in there with their employer until the fateful day because for the majority of people it is 'better the devil you know'. Hindsight, that most wonderful clarity, has now taught me that this is most certainly not always the case, as your loyalty is rarely rewarded these days, as you might have also come to realise.

For the last eight years of employed life, I kept taking on new and very different challenges, which resulted in my career going 'off piste' and away from the travel side of the business into specialist senior project and HR roles. At the time of the redundancy, I had inadvertently reinvented myself as Reward and Benefits Manager. From a standing start, I had built a strong reputation as a specialist and expert, especially in developing innovative new pay and reward schemes. The reality was once I had learned my trade and the challenge had worn off, I was becoming increasingly unhappy, unfulfilled and the continual changes at Board and Group level were making it almost impossible to get any project completed. This was becoming a major frustration for me and my team and made it easier for me to see through some of the cracks emerging in the company. However, I still stuck at it!

What I now realise is that, as you will see consistently throughout this book, what I did prove is that you can always learn new skills and reinvent yourself to make you more marketable. I didn't see it this way when redundancy hit and this might also be the case with you. Likewise, you would not believe the number of new clients who lament the fact that they are *'just a generalist'*. They have actually done many different roles within their organisations so feel they are disadvantaged, because it is hard to put them into an obvious 'box'. It is a rare person who does realise the true value of having developed his or her career by working in a multitude of different functions and business disciplines, albeit in the same organisation. What if your mindset shifted to thinking and believing that, by having a wide range of skills, being flexible and adaptable and embracing change, this would put you in good stead for many different types of jobs or even for starting a business of your own? Put this way, does the future suddenly not look infinitely more positive and appealing? I'm sure it does, so read on!

My wakeup call eventually came when the company decided to move all the Head Offices to a specially designed new group Head Quarters under one roof in the North of England. Whilst the company decision made complete commercial sense to me and I bore no ill feelings about this, I had some difficult decisions to make. For some people it might have been a fantastic opportunity to relocate and continue building their careers at an exciting time of change in the company.

It was a totally new experience for me and was to become a career defining moment in my life and therefore my decision was a no-brainer. Although I was offered the opportunity of an excellent job, the chance to relocate, afford a much grander house and live in relative luxury, I didn't want to uproot. It wasn't the right time for the family, especially with our kids coming up to their GCSE's. Equally, in such an uncertain economic climate what were the chances of more restructuring once we had settled and then I could be at even greater risk of losing my job? We would then have the decision whether to relocate back to the south and higher house prices or stay in an area we had never planned to live, creating even more stress, upheaval and uncertainty.

There were in fact a number of further restructures over the next eighteen months, so anything could have happened. More to the point, I quickly realised ***I didn't want somebody telling me how to lead my life, where I was going to live and feel I was beholden to the company for my future.*** I wanted to be in control of my life and career and this is what I now call 'being the architect of your own future'. I therefore decided to 'take the money and run'.

Little did I know that the resulting journey would have such a profound impact on my life and take my career in a completely different direction, helping me find and develop new passions to become an expert in the field of Career Development, Career Change and Transition and also a speaker and published author! I am forever grateful for the opportunity that redundancy provided and I know you will also come to feel the same way by the time you finish reading this book.

Outplacement

As part of my redundancy package, my company gave me the benefit of 'outplacement' support with a major career consultancy. This was a new word to me and it is not exactly the most user friendly term, but essentially is about providing moral and job search support to employees facing redundancy and equipping them with the tools and knowledge to give them a better and quicker chance of finding their next job.

Outplacement is one of the main services my company now provides and to my way of thinking (and our company ethos) should be about helping you to develop and manage your career but equally importantly, help you manage the emotional reactions of redundancy. Unfortunately, the reality is that the provision is somewhat hit and miss, because often organisations just want to be seen to be doing the honourable thing by their departing employees. The result is that the outplacement process becomes a 'tick box' exercise rather than meeting individual needs at such an uncertain and difficult time.

As a member of the senior management team, I was fortunate to be given the option of attending a self employment course and also doing some specialist personality profiling to help ascertain aspects of my behaviour, motivation, temperament, communication style, competencies, management capabilities and much more. These were most revealing and started to shape my thinking, consequently we will look at some different types of profiling in Chapter three and self employment in more detail in Chapter five.

The self employment course was undoubtedly the best part of the outplacement support. It proved to me that self employment was an option and rekindled previous ideas about running my own business. Probably like most people, the time had never seemed right or maybe it was just easier to stay in my comfort zone. Maybe you haven't realised this yet, but does this ring bells with you?

Interestingly, the work I did with my consultant highlighted a major career dilemma, which you may well face yourself, i.e. what was the best option for me. Should I:

- Aim to progress my career all over again in another similar company
- Look at reinventing my career in a completely different business sector

Or

- Look at a complete change and set up my own business?'

Being my own boss was definitely appealing, but there were some key questions to be answered i.e. what would I be the boss of? What would my business do? I had a number of ideas but nothing concrete. The kudos of a corporate executive position and the company benefits associated with it were equally attractive, but my dislike of company politics and time away from the family at constant (and often unnecessary) meetings was not!

How could I make my decision? If only I had a process to work through to help me. I know you may be feeling the same. The good news is this book has been specifically written with you in mind to take you on a voyage of self discovery and a proven process to guide you to make an effective decision. This is where I really needed the support but it was not forthcoming. I was given what I now know to be some of the worst possible career advice: '*Take the summer off and get your head straight and you will be in a much better position to move forward*'. This was wrong on so many counts, as I will explain in Chapter one.

We had a 'downsized' family holiday, then I found all sorts of non work related activities to fill my days that I never seemed to have time for when I was working such as; improve my golf, do some projects around the house, spend more time with my kids, some serious reading and just chilling out. The future should have been exciting but was scary and confusing and I did not know who to turn to or how to make my decision. What should I do for the best and what was right for me? I simply did not know how to go forward and I wonder d*oes this resonate with you?* My decision, like those of many other people I have since met, was not to make a decision and for the first time in my life, I descended into procrastination mode!

One Size Does Not Fit All

I saw how redundancy affected my colleagues and it became abundantly clear that people react differently, therefore in terms of support and guidance, one size does not fit all. This is a mantra that I now live by in my own business. Some colleagues were totally devastated and buried their heads in the sand, going into denial; others jumped ship immediately to get ahead of the competition. Then there were those who thought more about how they would spend some of their redundancy package; maybe treating the family to a special holiday, getting work done on their house or paying off the mortgage.

This shows clearly how differently people react and how diverse are their agendas, motivations and emotional reactions and these were rarely addressed. As a result, most of us battled on in blissful ignorance by ourselves, some jumping at the first job that came along, often out of the frying pan and into the fire, facing redundancy again in only a matter of months. Although I was confused, I always thought there must be a better way to support departing employees at such a difficult and emotional time. Little did I know that I would be starting to do just that a year later!

How Did I End Up Doing What I Do Now?

I get asked this question all the time. I suppose in a way it was a mixture of fate, accident and the Law of Attraction which we will be revisiting at various points in the book. Eventually, I found my salvation on a government sponsored programme that supports unemployed executives and professionals back to work with career and management development workshops and 1:1 support. This was run by an independent training and development company a couple of days a week over a number of weeks.

I turned up for my first workshop expecting to be in a small group of similarly 'lost souls' and this was true in so far as the majority had lost their way and were struggling to see the wood for the trees. What did surprise me was being part of a group of more than twenty largely talented executives who had been victims of redundancy from a wide range of sectors and professions. I felt reassured that I was not alone and it made me realise the importance of a support network, something that I cannot stress strongly enough. We will revisit this in Chapter one and again cover networking in more detail in Chapter four.

I quickly realised that, like many of my former work colleagues, this group had reacted to their situations in very different ways. Like me, some of them really wanted to work, but had lost confidence and were struggling. Others had lots of enthusiasm and confidence but were clueless about job searching or how to market themselves and were applying for every job they saw. Also, there was the negative brigade who I recognised as a hard core of people who had developed a negative attitude about every aspect of their situation. They were in denial, bitter and twisted and were determined to rubbish the course. Despite this, they still thought they had a divine right to secure a similar job to the one they had before, but without the hard graft. I will allude to the importance and impact of mindset in Chapter one and throughout the book. A few had even lost the desire to work altogether and were biding their time on benefits until they claimed their pensions. You couldn't blame them. However, I have since come to realise that this was a missed opportunity for them to try something different. They could have used the opportunity to discover something they love doing to keep mind and body active, rather than retiring completely, which is often the death knell for so many people.

I quickly found renewed energy, enthusiasm and confidence and for the first time in nearly a year the clouds started to lift and I could start to see things more clearly. I was finding a new lease of life and sense of purpose. Although the course was good, I could see lots of ways in which it could be improved and I was really starting to feel in tune with the career development work. This created a sense of excitement of being able to make a positive contribution. I could see a potential opportunity to utilise my previous management and people development skills. With my confidence renewed, I offered the Managing Director of the training consultancy some constructive suggestions to improve the programme. I could see by changing the tone from teaching to adopting a more facilitative and coaching approach, it would make the course much more engaging and interactive, which I believe is really important to aid learning. One of the most important learning points for me was the new concept of 'the portfolio career'. This is a massive mindset shift from having a job to earning income from different business strands, skills and ideally interests and passions. This was really appealing and we will cover this in more depth in later Chapters of the book. The portfolio career concept has helped to transform my life, as well as that of many of my clients and other people I have met. Although it may not seem to be the case to you right now, I learnt that you do have CHOICE and I know that when you also come to this realisation, you will have reached a key turning point!

I now had the motivation and self belief to set up my own business, although I was still not clear what that business was going to look like. However, I did have some consultancy work already lined up in the Reward and Benefits arena and was keen to develop a portfolio career utilising skills I had developed over many years, a range of business interests including embracing my new passion for Career Development. Most importantly I was determined to take action and make it happen and you will see this is key to Chapter six.

I finished the programme on the first anniversary of my late father's birthday with an absolute commitment to sign off at the Job Centre, never to sign on again. I formally set up as self employed and so that I would never forget the day I dedicated my business (SMP Solutions) in his honour. As they say, the rest is history!

The MD of the training company asked me to make a cameo appearance at the next executive course to share with the group why I had chosen to set up my own business. As a result of the positive feedback from this first venture, I was invited to run a half day workshop. I then graduated to training a variety of full day workshops and providing 1:1 career advice and guidance support. In addition, I took another massive leap of faith by volunteering my services (albeit partly paid) to help the consultancy rewrite the whole career development programme. This evolved further as I became their lead trainer in four locations and also helped to mentor and train new trainers. I was *becoming the architect of my own future*. With the help of this book, you can become the architect of your own wonderful future too!

The Power Of Passion

My new journey had well and truly begun and it was both exciting and scary, nonetheless, I was determined that I was never going to look back. What became apparent was that the more passionate I felt about the work I was doing, the more the work started coming my way. The power of this cannot be underestimated! We will be exploring some of the 'Universal Laws of Success and Achievement' in more detail in Chapter five of the book.

Since achieving my own successful career transition, I have devoted the last ten years of my life to becoming an expert in the field of Outplacement, Career Change and Career Development. I am more passionate than ever about making a difference and helping people win through redundancy. I do this by coaching you through a process which will give you the 'tools' to change your mindset and beliefs. Although this might be a difficult and challenging time of your life, wouldn't it be great to realise you are never too old to make a successful career change to end up doing work you love and lead a fulfilling life? That would be really empowering and liberating, wouldn't it?

People tell me that my passion becomes infectious, which is why so much of my business comes from recommendations and referrals and wouldn't you want to work with someone who shows real enthusiasm, commitment, interest and passion for what they do? I will be constantly referring to the power of passion throughout this book. If you have never thought it possible that you **can** do work that you love, I would like to plant this seed with you now. *Why?* Because almost anything is possible with the right mindset, positive beliefs and positive actions!

Navigate Your Way To Success

Having finally achieved a successful career change myself and having seen what worked and what didn't, I was determined to make it easier for other people to make a winning career transition following redundancy. And I wanted to make sure that it would be easier regardless of their situation, length of career or level they had worked at. Since then I've worked with thousands of clients over the last decade and established the common themes for successful career transition and change. When I analysed these, plus also considered my own journey post redundancy, I discovered that there is a definite process to achieve a successful evolution. With this in mind, I developed the 'SMP Career Navigation Cycle' which will be referred to henceforth as 'The Career Navigation Cycle' or 'the Cycle', and I have used it successfully with thousands of people in a variety of situations over many years.

The Cycle works in almost every conceivable situation providing you have had a reasonable career with at least a few years of paid employment. The process is even stronger following redundancy when emotions are running much higher. It is much easier to become derailed without a practical structure and process to work through to keep you focused and on track.

One of my few unfulfilled life goals, until now, has been to write a book that will have a positive impact on people and make a difference to their lives. This is my opportunity to influence you by taking you through each step of my Cycle,

Chapter by Chapter, helping you to reach a successful conclusion to *win through redundancy and navigate your way to a brighter future* and most importantly end up doing work you love.

Career Navigation Cycle

Career Navigation Cycle Overview Of Each Step

Step 1 – Let go and look forward

You are what you think and feel. To tackle any major change you have to change your thinking – you have to learn to look forward not back

Step 2 – Re-evaluate

What is important to you in your career and life and WHY?

Step 3 – Establish your true marketability

Know who you are and what you have to offer – your 'complete package'

Step 4 – Explore Opportunities

Research, network, find and evaluate new opportunities

Step 5 – Decide what to do

Follow your passions; know what you want and where to find it

Step 6 – Take positive action

The future may look scary or exciting. Either way you must follow through with your career action plan to succeed!

Health Warning...

My aim is purposefully very different to many other career books. My approach is to combine the power of Personal Development with practical Career Development strategies to help you combat the psychological and emotional responses to redundancy and career change to turn the threat into a real opportunity. See my Career Navigation Cycle diagram split into two halves on page 37.

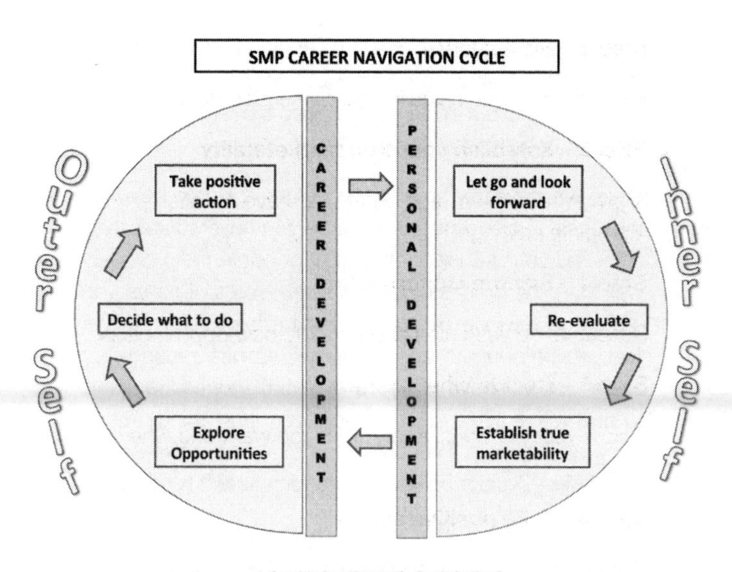

Steps 1-3 of the Cycle are integral to your ultimate success, because this is where the hard graft and real inner self, soul searching work that most people rarely do, takes place. By putting in the effort in these Chapters you will be well positioned to set yourself up for a fulfilling career and life, providing you then continue to build momentum working through the rest of the Chapters and Steps of the Cycle. The final Chapters, Steps 4-6 of the Cycle are outer self work and contain much more in the way of practical career development activities, practical tips and case studies to help you complete the Cycle and achieve a successful outcome.

It is important to follow through each step of the Cycle, not skipping any of it, as there is a logical sequence to the process. You need to go through this Cycle, follow it right round and then you will come through the 'other side' having learnt a huge amount about yourself. The process is like anything in life i.e. you have to put in the effort to get the reward. *There is no magic wand, there is no holy grail*, so you have to put in the effort to reap the return. You reap what you sow as the saying goes.

There will inevitably be crossover along the way. Likewise the Cycle is also virtuous as once you have successfully achieved your transition, it is very possible that you may well start the process again in a few years' time as you grow and develop personally and professionally. Also, if you are unfortunate enough to experience redundancy again, you will have a tried and tested process to revert to and follow. This will help you kick start things much more quickly, with the confidence of knowing the Career Navigation Cycle process worked for you first time round.

Having established this is the right book for you, you are now ready to start work on your career transition and turn your redundancy into a brave new world of opportunity. The process is very individual. There is no set timescale. For some people it can be days to work your way round, for others, weeks and some (including me) it was months. However, I did not have the benefit of the insights which you will have by reading this book. You may already realise that the impact of redundancy can be an emotional roller coaster ride, but I will make sure it also becomes a great voyage of self discovery for you.

Fasten your seatbelt and enjoy the journey!

CHAPTER 1

Let Go And Look Forward – Step 1

"Your past does not equal nor does it dictate your future... Focus on where you want to go, not what you fear"

Anthony Robbins, Entrepreneur,
Author & Peak Performance Strategist

As a result of your redundancy you are at a career crossroads and starting on a voyage of self discovery. To *navigate your way to a brighter future* you will need to overcome hurdles, roadblocks and a myriad of other obstacles that can come your way. Unless you are very lucky, it is inevitable there will be some, so be prepared and I will do my best to steer you on the right course to a positive outcome.

Whatever stage you are at with your redundancy and for whatever reasons you are attracted to this book, the starting point for any successful career transition is to *'let go and look forward'*. This can be a real 'tug of war' so think of your situation as *'work in progress'*.

In this Chapter we will explore:

- Your perspective – what is your outlook right now?
- Embracing change – are you willing to accept that change must happen?
- Practical tips when facing redundancy – how to stay ahead of the game
- The 'emotional roller coaster' – managing the ride and your emotions
- Personal Development – ways to develop a 'toolkit of knowledge' to be the best you can be
- Mindset – how you can change your thinking, to change your life
- Fear and Focus – how not to let your fear paralyse you
- The Law of Attraction – how you can attract positive outcomes

Perspective – What Does Letting Go Mean To You?

To start your journey, you need to consider where you are coming from right now. Is this from a position of:

- Trauma
- Feeling of failure
- The victim
- Shock
- Despair
- Anger
- Denial
- Depression
- Fear
- Frustration
- Happiness
- Relief
- Focus
- Opportunity

The aim of this Chapter is to move you to a desired state of **belief in the Career Navigation Cycle process** to let go and look forward. Consider the PERSPECTIVE acronym and spend a few minutes quietly thinking through what these statements mean to you. As you work your way through the book you will develop and experience these aspects as you navigate each step of the Cycle.

P = *Purposeful focus on your new future*

E = *Enlightenment as you embark on a journey*

R = *Realise and release your potential*

S = *Self-reflection to build self-belief*

P = *Positive attitude, beliefs and mindset*

E = *Evolving process to achieve your goal*

C = *Create and implement a plan*

T = *Transformational experience*

I = *Imagine limitless possibilities*

V = *Visualise and feel your success*

E = *Evaluate all options and enjoy the process*

Time For Change

"It is not the strongest of the species that survives, nor the most intelligent, but the one most responsive to change."

Charles Darwin, Scientist & Naturalist, 1809-1882

We know change is one of life's certainties but what most of us cannot accept is change for change sake. However, most change happens as a result of external factors e.g. the economy, competitive pressures, market forces, new technology and so on. Whatever the sector, businesses and organisations must constantly evolve, reinvent themselves and look forward to thrive and survive. **You** are no different. The point I am making is you will not stop the march of change or progress. However, as with most things in life you have two options:

1. See your situation as a threat, negative, resist change, feel you are a victim and fight a constantly frustrating and ultimately losing battle

Or

2. See your situation as an opportunity to embrace change, re-evaluate your career and life, learn and ultimately reap the rewards to create a working lifestyle you want!

It is hard for us to keep up with the pace of such dramatic changes, especially in technology and communications. However, it is essential you keep learning and adapting, as this will help you in your quest to achieve a successful career transition.

Imagine life without your Smartphone!

We have all learnt to use these devices to maintain contact with friends, colleagues, web browsing, forums etc. and we would now be lost without them. Also, access to Social Media has emerged from nowhere over the past few years. Like it or not, Social Media is here to stay. It is also evolving and having an ever greater impact on our lives. I'm sure you know people who cannot get through the day without their daily 'fix' of Facebook or Twitter, don't you?

Social Media is also having a dramatic impact on the world of work, recruitment, networking and job searching, which we will explore in more detail in Chapter 4. I meet many people who are resisting such an important revolution but ignore this at your peril if you are a serious career professional. Embracing social media is a classic example of where you need to be open to change. A contact of mine told me of a situation where he was being interviewed for a new job and the HR manager expressed a major concern, as they could not find him on any social networks. The suggestion was that either he was well hidden or a luddite! This was a sharp reality check and needless to say he didn't get the job.

Practical Tips If You Are *Facing* Redundancy

There are many things you will want to know if you are facing redundancy. A good employer should help you with most of the key things you must know regarding your redundancy pay, any extra package and what happens with your pension if you have a company scheme. From personal experience, supporting thousands of clients over the last decade, there are some other very important tips you may not be told, that could make a significant difference to you personally or help get you ahead of the game.

1. **Be prepared for your exit** - Too many people don't take any action until they leave their job then go into panic mode. If the writing is on the wall, be proactive so you are in control. This book will help.

2. **Know your rights -** Don't assume your employer will get things right or always do things 'by the book'. I have come across many examples where people have been 'screwed over' by their employer without them realising until they told me about their situation. Even large organisations with a strong HR presence have been known to try to shortcut the process or not follow correct policy or procedures for redundancy selection. If in doubt seek independent advice e.g. from your Union, if you have one, or external support organisations such as ACAS, or Citizens Advice, who can provide invaluable impartial advice. You may have an Employee Assistance helpline, but be mindful this is often closely aligned to your HR department, so not totally independent. Also, if you have legal cover

on your home insurance, you are likely to be covered for legal expenses in relation to supporting a claim you may have against your employer for any 'wrong doing', which could result in an Employment Tribunal. Don't leave anything to chance!

3. **You may be able to negotiate terms -** Don't assume your 'package' is set in tablets of stone. Depending on your seniority, years of service, the financial position of the organisation or their redundancy budget, you may be able to influence a better deal. Any additional improvement you can gain over your statutory or proposed redundancy agreement will help you at this difficult time.

4. **Outplacement support** - I know from my experience of providing outplacement services and support to employers, sometimes they work on a 'need to know basis'. Therefore, they may have a budget for support but if you don't ask you don't get, so ask the question! Your employer may offer you a programme of support with their 'preferred providers'. The point here is that you often get a bog standard 'one size fits all' service which is rather impersonal. Many of my clients negotiate a budget for their support then insist on spending it with my company, as they know they will get the individual support they want, rather than what their employer wants them to have because it is the easy option. Regardless, try to make sure you get some support as something is better than nothing at all.

5. **Compromise agreements -** This is a legally binding agreement which brings your employment to an end. In return for an agreed package, you, in turn, agree to keep confidentiality in relation to your departure and to waive any opportunity to take legal action against your employer. However, to maximise the opportunity

you must make sure you are in control. Employers are now increasingly using compromise agreements as a mechanism for preventing possible future complaints to an employment tribunal. Therefore, taking into account point 3, you may have some key negotiating ammunition, depending on the reasons for the compromise.

6. **Leave on good terms -** However you are feeling about your redundancy, don't 'cut off your nose to spite your face'. Be professional right to the last as you might want a reference, recommendation or introduction from your employer, your boss, another manager or colleague within the organisation. Also, it is a very small world and what goes around comes around - managing your reputation is a key part of your personal brand, which we will explore in Chapter three.

7. **Take advantage of any outplacement support offered** - If your employer offers you the opportunity for outplacement, then take it! I have all too often seen employees who refuse outplacement as an act of defiance to their employer. Never be too proud, or think of outplacement as belittling you, as the only person who loses out is you! If your employer is prepared to support your exit, take any help you can get as it could fast track you into your next job plus you never know when you might need to use the learning again. Timing can be all important. If you are coming up to the organisation's financial year end, often budgets must be spent otherwise you won't get access to this pot of money again.

   Some examples of negotiated extra benefits from clients I have worked with are:

- A higher payout in the form of a retention bonus for staying to the bitter end

- Leaving immediately to go on 'gardening leave' whilst being paid your notice entitlement so you can start working on your new life
- Additional payment in lieu of notice
- A sum of money for your outplacement support if not offered
- Additional budget for outplacement to provide for a higher level of support, or longer programme
- Other developmental training to help you achieve a qualification or to up skill for something which will benefit you either in the short or longer term

8. **Should you sign on at your local Jobcentre?** - Dependent on your redundancy package and financial situation, you may or may not be entitled to any Job Seekers benefits. Legislation around this is constantly changing so you must check this out. You may feel disinclined to put yourself through this humiliating process, especially if you don't want to be constantly questioned about your job search activity, while you are working your way through this book. However, bear in mind you will be entitled to claim National Insurance (NI) credits once you have received your final payment from your employer. If you are still out of work at this stage and signed on, the government in effect becomes your employer and pays your NI. This saves you having a gap in NI payments, which has caused many people much frustration and hassle sorting out the red tape further down the line. You may also be entitled to funding for specific training courses you cannot afford or do not wish to pay for yourself. Be aware that funding is constantly changing.

Managing Your Emotions

Everyone is affected differently by redundancy. For many it is highly traumatic, similar to bereavement as one of the most stressful situations any one of us may have to face in life. How you manage your emotions will play a big part in how quickly you can *let go and look forward*. Say to yourself: '*It's not about me*.' Difficult as it may seem, try not to take your redundancy personally. There is almost always an underlying reason for the redundancies e.g. the general economic climate, market conditions, the need to cut costs, reduce headcount and manpower, outsourcing, restructuring etc.

The Emotional Roller Coaster

There are many change curves and models illustrating what can happen to you as a result of loss or key change in your life. However, I want you to imagine you are on a roller coaster ride with **upward, downward and sideways swings**, as it is rarely the case you will have straight downward then upward swings. Your journey is likely to be an *'emotional roller coaster'* but how you manage your emotions through the ride is what counts.

If you have never experienced redundancy, it is helpful to understand how the loss of your job may affect you and what you can do to turn this negative situation into a positive outcome for you. There are five main impacts, which can be dramatically exaggerated when redundancy is very sudden or totally unexpected:

- Shock, denial and anger – **why me?**
- Fear of the unknown – **will I get another job, can I survive financially?**

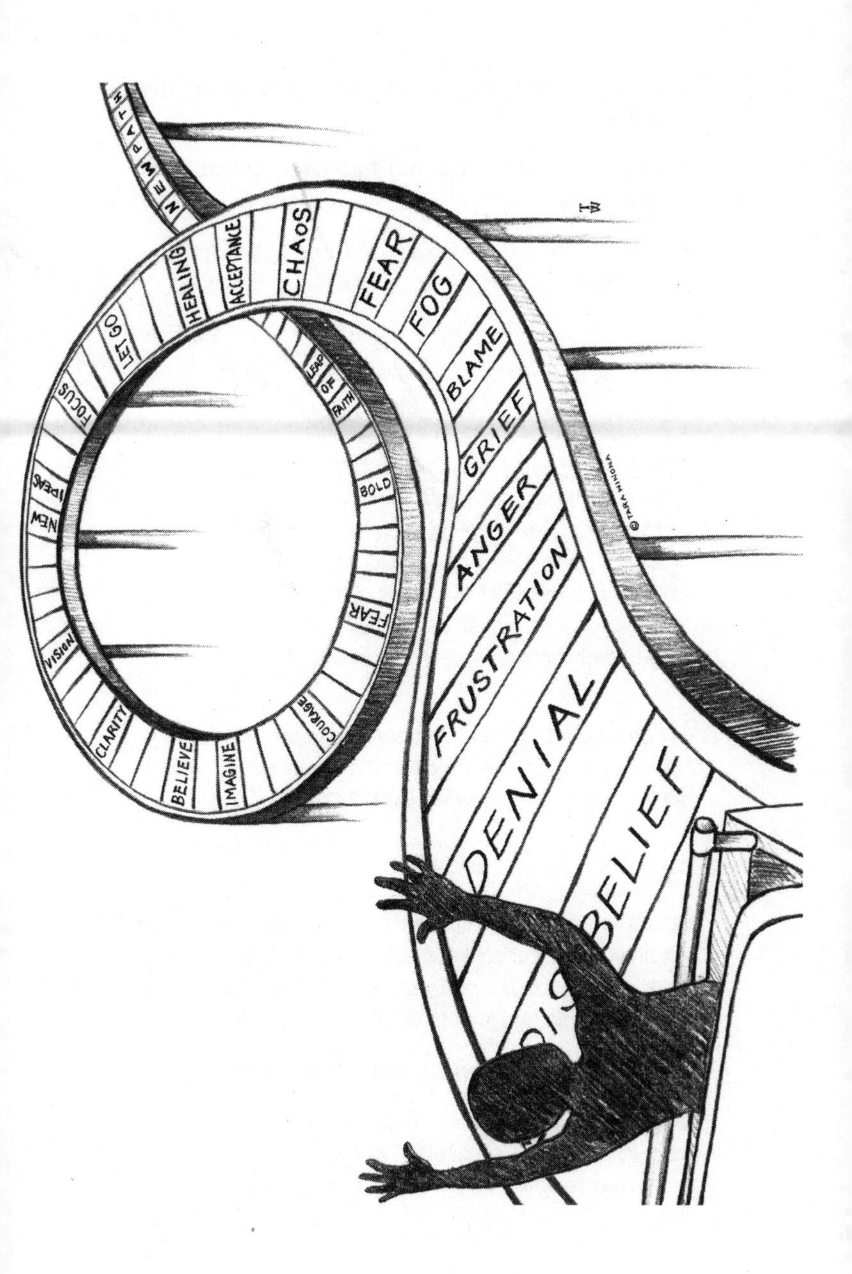
NEW PATH
FOCUS
LET GO
HEALING
ACCEPTANCE
CHAOS
FEAR
FOG
BLAME
GRIEF
ANGER
FRUSTRATION
DENIAL
DISBELIEF
NEW IDEAS
VISION
CLARITY
BELIEVE
IMAGINE
COURAGE
FEAR
BOLD
LEAP OF FAITH

- Loss of confidence and self esteem – **do I have any value?**
- Loss of control – **'the rug has been pulled from under me'**
- Loss of structure - **how will I cope without any routine?**

Health Warning... There Is No Right Or Wrong Way To Feel

There are so many individual factors which can affect your thinking e.g. the questions we looked at in the introduction. For some people (especially if you are in line for a good payout) there might be an initial feeling of euphoria followed by crashing down to earth and some of the above, as happened to me. This again clearly highlights *'one size does not fit all'*.

The ***Emotional Roller Coaster*** illustrates what many people go through when experiencing redundancy. *Where are you on the roller coaster ride right now?*

Coping Strategies – Do's

Regardless of your situation and how you may be feeling, I will share with you some effective strategies to help you move safely round the ***Emotional Roller Coaster*** to ultimately 'let go and look forward'.

Allow yourself to be upset and grieve... for a while!

Redundancy is constantly highlighted as one of the most stressful life situations, along with close family bereavements and divorce. In all of these situations there is a cocktail of emotions involved, especially in being able to let go of the past. There is inevitably always a grieving period, after which the first step to letting go and looking forward is acceptance.

By all means grieve for your job if you enjoyed it but you must start to think and act differently. Redundancy is not the same as bereavement, as no one has passed on. Maybe it is more like a divorce, as there has been a parting of a bond. However, as with divorce, as painful as it might be in the build-up and aftermath, there is still life ahead of you. People can and do move on and start a new life, so there is no reason why you can't either, is there?

Regroup - Start to see your redundancy as an opportunity!

At this stage you might be thinking it is easy for me to say this but how do I get myself to a better place? Don't worry, as most of this Chapter will cover exercises, strategies, practical tips and case studies to start to help you think differently, so that you can start to let go and look forward and ultimately see your redundancy in a new light. Also, there is always light at the end of the tunnel isn't there?

Live your dream – do what you want to!

Redundancy might be the first time in your life you have the opportunity to take stock and review what **you** really want to do with your career and life. Rather than feeling obligated to do 'more of the same', embrace your voyage of self discovery to live your dreams so you end up doing work **you want and love**! You also have an opportunity to revisit any 'what if' thoughts you may have had from the past e.g. what if I set up my own business, what if I change career to become…?

Manage your career change as a project - make the journey step by step

From now on, treat your career transition as a project and you will be far more successful. You **are** a work in progress, *'between jobs, exploring new opportunities.'* As things start to evolve, you can set aims, objectives, milestones and outcomes which you can constantly review and revise to keep you on track to achieve your end goal. As with many things in life, what gets measured gets done!

Talk to people - it's good to talk!

Don't forget there are always other people who have trodden the path before you. If you have never experienced redundancy before, it pays to talk to people who have and got through the other side and are now thriving. What did they do and learn? I will be sharing my experiences with you and case studies of other people, but it is likely you also know people who have been in your situation. Find them and talk things through. You never know what may come from this.

Believe most people genuinely want to help!

Taking my last point, so often I have heard people say 'I didn't want to bother so and so as I know they are always busy'. Do yourself a favour and change your beliefs around this, as the majority of people are only too pleased to help if they can. This is something I learnt very early on in my transition, which was a very pleasant surprise. Why do most people want to help? Simple... human nature being what it is, people don't like to see you unhappy or disadvantaged and they also might consider how they would like people to react if they were in your position. Therefore, if they can help in any way they mostly will, with the caveat from my list of don'ts i.e. 'don't dump your baggage on others'!

Get independent financial advice

If you have come away with a good redundancy payout you should seek advice from a trusted or recommended source to determine the best options to manage your personal finances. You may also want to do the same for your pension, if you have one. We will revisit the importance of this when re-evaluating your finances in Chapter two.

Get the right support networks - surround yourself with positive people!

We will explore the importance of a positive mindset in detail in this Chapter. The key here is positive people radiate positive energy, which becomes infectious. Now is the time you need positive energy by the bucket load, so you need to be around positive people who will boost you up rather than bring you down. Bear in mind it may not always be your nearest and dearest. Even if they are full of empathy, sympathy and well meaning, they are sometimes (not always) way too close and if they are overly fearful for the future, they may hinder rather than help you. My experience has proven it is often the most unlikely people who can help unlock the key to your future. Think about who are the valued and trusted contacts you have made throughout your career and your networks in general? Now is the time to start rebuilding and developing your networks both online and offline. We will revisit the importance of networks and networking throughout the book, especially in Step 4 of the Cycle when 'exploring opportunities'.

Celebrate 'small wins'

Following your redundancy it is important to look for 'small wins', so you can see you are making progress towards your goal. This might be making new connections, starting to let go, feeling more confident, or getting invited to interviews. Despite any knock backs always take the learning out of any situation, constantly focusing on moving towards your end goal. For each 'small win' why not give yourself a small 'reward' of something you have held back on e.g. a meal out, some 'retail therapy', a bottle of wine or something to make you feel good and positive about yourself. Be proud, as you are making progress and that should feel good, don't you think?

Personal Development

"If you wish to achieve worthwhile things in your personal and career life, you must become a worthwhile person in your own self development"

Brian Tracy, Professional Speaker, Best Selling Author, Entrepreneur and Success Expert

Many people feel that by getting more professional qualifications it will help them in their career. This depends entirely on what you are planning to do next and the relevance of the qualifications gained. I have met many people who have invested large sums of money on their professional development only to find it took them up a blind alley. However, working on your personal development will help you for the rest of your life, regardless of what you do. We will be looking at ways to develop and grow personally, useful materials to motivate and inspire you and looking at relevant professional help for your needs.

Work On Your Personal Development & Growth

Think of Personal Development like going to the gym but instead of developing your muscles you are developing your mind. Finding the tools and materials that work best for you will help you learn how to develop a successful mindset, improve your confidence and self esteem and become the best person you can be. Imagine how this will impact positively on your outlook on life and likewise your career? How good would this be? I have provided some useful tips to help you on your way:

Reading inspiring material (like this book), listening to personal development CD's, MP3 files, attending motivational workshops, seminars and courses can all help to inspire you, teach you new skills, learn success strategies and change your thinking to help you let go and look forward. I don't believe in harbouring regrets but wonder how my life would have shaped up if I had learnt some of these key strategies when I was younger. At least I can now share them with family, friends, my clients and of course you!

One of my all time favourite audio books is *The New Psychology of Achievement* by world renowned psychologist, author, speaker and success guru, Brian Tracy. I personally love Brian Tracy for his amazing ability to translate highly complex aspects of psychology into simple practical solutions to achieve success in your life. Brian Tracy's audio programmes and work have acted as a mentor to me, providing me with great insight, which has inspired and influenced me personally and also many of my clients, with whom I have shared his work.

Another book I recommend highly is '*Who Moved My Cheese*' by Dr Spencer Johnson: an amazingly clever book which uses cheese as a metaphor for what you want to have in life. It is just under 100 pages so you can read it cover to cover in no time. The book has achieved 'cult' status with organisations and individuals around the globe, as people are drawn to stories with metaphors as a way of learning to manage change and build self esteem.

I have also learnt that a key factor in achieving personal success is to take some risks which push you out of your comfort zone. People who have high self esteem take risks and people who take risks have high self esteem. We will be revisiting this throughout the book.

To summarise the power of personal development, in the words of the late, great Jim Rohn (psychologist and mentor to Tony Robbins) *"One of the keys to a successful life is to work harder on yourself than you do on your job. Working on your job will earn your living whereas working on yourself can earn you a fortune!"*

Get Professional Help – Hire A Career Coach It Will Pay You!

This book will help you coach yourself and will be a brilliant guide to *winning through redundancy and navigating your way to a brighter future.* However, a good career coach can support all the good work you will do in this book. They will act as a catalyst for your change to manage the emotional responses of redundancy, challenge you and your thinking, get you focused, unlock your potential and hidden talents so you can build a vision for your future, boost your confidence, keep you motivated and on track to achieve your goals.

Friends and family and other valued contacts are important to help you through this difficult transition. However, a good Career Coach, besides being an expert, is also independent and impartial. Therefore they can support you without the same emotional connection. The benefits they can provide to you will have a knock on effect to your family and support networks in general, as they see you become more positive, focused and moving forward with a real sense of purpose. Consider working with a Career Coach as a positive investment in your future. You are far more likely to make a speedier career change or transition, so will earn back the money you paid out much quicker to get a return on your investment. Alternatively, if you enjoy learning online in your own time and at your own pace, you may wish to consider investing in online career change programmes such as my innovative *'I Want A Career Change'* to support this book and your career transition journey. Details can be found in the *Useful and Inspiring Resources* pages.

Seek Counselling

If your redundancy has left you traumatised and you cannot cope or focus on anything. If you feel in total despair and are suffering from severe depression, you may need specialist help from a qualified counsellor before you can start your career transition journey and any self-exploration work. Your current or previous employer may even offer this service if they have an Employee Assistance scheme. Always check first before you seek external help, you might as well take advantage of any benefits on offer.

Getting Into The Right Mindset

Looking back on your life and career, I can pretty much guarantee that when things went well you had a positive mindset and you were determined to succeed. Winning through redundancy is no different - it is all about having the right mindset! Success guru, Brian Tracy says in his *New Psychology of Achievement* audio book, *"You always perform on the outside based on the way you think about yourself on the inside. You become what you think about most of the time. Change your thinking and you change your life"*. We will be exploring much about the importance of mindset and changing your thinking throughout this book, as it is key to your successful career transition and success in life.

Health Warning...

If you are looking to make a total career change, you are unlikely to have much of the information or tools you need at this early step of the Cycle. However, the Career Navigation Cycle process is designed to challenge your thinking and to give you a real sense of purpose. Following the natural flow of steps will help you to evolve, develop and refine your plan as you progress round the Cycle, to develop the winning mindset.

Reframe Your Thinking To Respond Differently

My years as a Career Coach have taught me that the nature of my previous work and the skills I acquired are relevant and in demand in pretty much any sector. People often become blinkered, so don't see the bigger picture of their transferable skills and true marketability (we will explore this in Chapter three). Your inherent talents and developed skills mean that there are always new opportunities and possibilities to be explored. Remember just because you have always done something or similar jobs before doesn't mean you can't do anything else. You always have a CHOICE!

I remember speaking at a major careers event for the medical profession. My theme was around challenging yourself to be open to new opportunities outside of the medical profession in light of the changing Health Service agenda. I had a queue of people waiting to see me after the seminar. One was a GP who was looking most concerned. He told me he had only ever been a GP so how could he possibly do anything else? Conscious of the long queue, waiting patiently, I asked a key question to help him on the way; 'Do you want to continue working with people?' The look of shock and horror on his face was unbelievable 'God no, I hate people!' He was clearly in the wrong job and may not have realised it before, but he started his career transition journey there and then.

The good news is that it is never too late to change career. What you can and must do is to reframe and take your positive learning and experiences from the past and bring these with you to help you move forward. When you combine these with a positive mindset, you have a winning combination. I'm sure this sounds more encouraging, doesn't it?

Controlling Your Own Self Talk & Inner Dialogue

Reframing your thinking will also make you aware of what you say and how you say it. I learnt very early on in my transition about the importance of positive language and the power of communication. Learning to manage and control your inner dialogue (what you are thinking and saying to yourself) is a key part of the reframing process.

Having now gained an understanding of the importance of your mindset and reframing, do you see your current career situation and life as a threat or an opportunity? Ask yourself this key question:

Are you behaving like a 'victim'; constantly bemoaning your fate to everyone you meet, so life passes you by like being an extra in your own movie?

Or

Do you see yourself as being the architect of your own new future, playing the starring role in your own movie, taking control of your career and making it happen? I'm sure you will agree this sounds much more appealing, doesn't it?

The importance of what you say, how you say it and to whom

The way you communicate plays a significant part in winning through redundancy and ultimately achieving a successful career change or transition. You never know who will unlock the key to your future, as I have mentioned and will continue to do so throughout the book. Communication becomes all important when networking (we will cover this in step 4), at interviews or for any informal interactions with people you meet in any situation. Remember, you never get a second chance to make a first impression, so make sure it is the right one for you!

Let's say you meet someone socially and they ask, '*what do you do*'? Do you say '*I am unemployed or I've been made redundant*' then proceed to tell them about your woes? If so, this is not uncommon in my experience. Instead, try hard to change your thinking and replace such comments with ***'I am between jobs and exploring new opportunities'.***

Let's say you were in IT. You could reframe your statement to '*I am an IT Manager. Due to restructuring, my role was made redundant. However, in all honesty it was time to move on and I am now looking for a new challenge*'. I'm sure you would rather help this person, wouldn't you?

Adopting a positive mindset and reframing your thinking means that you are far more likely to use positive language and gain a helpful response. Listen to the way you speak to others and notice their reaction. This will speak volumes about how you may need to change your language and tone to gain your desired reaction or response. Ask friends and family for honest feedback in helping you to identify any negative words or phrases that you may be using. Then make a list and try reframing them into positive ones. The following case study is an excellent example of how you can achieve this.

Dee's Story

Dee is a very talented lady who is highly memorable for many reasons. She was the very first client we had on our funded workshops for unemployed professionals and executives a few years ago. As soon as she arrived her personality lit up the room. She was clearly excited at the prospect of the workshop, came across as very bubbly, personable, intelligent and had some wonderfully creative ideas. Unfortunately, her ideas were being quashed by many of the people around her. This was seriously damaging her confidence, self-esteem and causing her to question her ability and beliefs. Dee left the workshop really motivated and determined to get her career back on track. I felt with the right support and guidance she would be a star!

A year later she resurfaced after a job abroad did not work out and things had gone from bad to worse. Her marriage had been a disaster and she had given up her career to play the dutiful housewife. She was now in her early thirties, single, living at home again and it was two years since she had had a proper job. Dee could not see the wood for the trees; her confidence and self worth were shot to pieces. She was determined to get her career and life back on track and borrowed the money from her parents to invest in her future with a coaching programme, which you can only admire her for. This made me even more determined to help her succeed!

Dee made excellent progress from the career coaching. She was energised, wanted to make up for lost time and the creative ideas were starting to flow again. She really associated with my Career Navigation Cycle process and was keen to unlock her potential, her passions and establish her true marketability to find work she loved. What struck me was how she would make a positive statement then almost immediately doubt herself using negative language and **"but"** time and again. What was her problem? Dee admitted she was struggling with her 'self talk'. Although outwardly trying to be positive, the voice in her head was challenging her which resulted in negative statements flowing forth. This was not surprising considering what she had been through. You may also be experiencing similar issues, so you will be pleased to know there is a solution.

I got Dee to focus on controlling self talk by practising disciplining herself to reframe the negative inner voice as soon as she felt it coming. Also, to listen very closely to what she was saying, how this was coming across and how people reacted to what she said. Experts suggest it takes 30 days to **break a habit** through sustained reframing and effort and she was up for the challenge! Eventually Dee managed to discipline and self coach herself so she could stop the negative self talk as soon as she felt it coming on. You would see her smile which acknowledged she had managed to take control of her inner dialogue. The impact was amazing and her language changed completely with excitement replacing self doubts. It was a joy talking with her on the phone. She would tell me about all the exciting things that were happening to her and seemed bemused at why this was suddenly the case.

What Dee failed to recognise was that her new positive focus and vibrant energy was manifesting more of what she wanted in her life instead of what she didn't want, as you will read about shortly in the Law of Attraction. Good things started to happen for her and she quickly started turning her life around. She is now focusing on doing work she loves, developing a portfolio career - trading commodities, Forex trading, property development and even some temporary work. And also has become engaged!

Don'ts

The following list is to help you avoid slipping into a negative mindset, which will only lead you to doubt yourself as did Dee.

1. Don't live in the past – *"You cannot recreate the past but you can create a great new future"*

Living in the past will achieve nothing, other than causing pain and frustration, as you can no longer influence the past. You may have been very happy in your job but your redundancy has affected the way you feel. You might have thought you were up for promotion but have been laid off instead or you were expecting a move to a different department and job as part of the restructure, but it was not to be.

If you have already left, following redundancy, you might be missing the colleagues you worked with for a number of years and the daily banter and interaction. This can often be difficult to replace quickly if at all. You may have been a 'victim' of your employer going bust or having to close down due to the impact of the recession. Even worse, you may have suffered some form of discrimination, bullying or harassment which has resulted in your situation becoming untenable, so you were forced into a decision about leaving and maybe taking legal action against your employer.

Sadly, I have an increasing number of clients in this situation, which says much about today's workplace and culture. If you are unfortunate enough to have been in such a situation, this understandably leaves you with a bad taste and highly negative feelings towards your employer and sometimes emotional scars. This can be especially true if your situation has resulted in legal action, which can be a highly stressful, all consuming and often lengthy process.

It is easy to blame your company, your boss, the government, the bankers or whoever else you feel negative towards if you are frustrated at losing your job when you least expected it. As I highlighted earlier, you are entitled to feel aggrieved and negative about your situation at first but try not to dwell on this, as the quicker you can let go and look forward the better.

2. Don't 'beat yourself up'

Let's not beat about the bush. Unless you were hoping for redundancy as an escape route and to come away with some money, you may be upset. The key is to understand that there is a grieving process. If you follow the rest of these strategies it will help you 'let go and look forward', as quickly as possible, bearing in mind we are all different.

So many of my clients say to me: '*I don't understand why I am feeling this way, as I am usually a very positive person*'. My typical answer is '*what you are describing is a natural reaction to what has happened to you*'. You never asked for this situation, so it is understandable you may feel unhappy, bitter, frustrated, vengeful and fearful and any other amount of negative emotions, especially if you experienced some of the situations highlighted earlier in this Chapter. The important thing is not to 'beat yourself up' over this.

Another important consideration is you may get 'waves of emotion', just like any other grieving process, so just when you thought you had let go, other emotions come back to haunt you. Many people will experience an emotional roller coaster but accept this and learn to ride it out.

3. Don't dump your 'baggage' on other people!

It might be a difficult time for you but most people don't want to hear all your woes of the world. If you are constantly projecting a negative persona, people won't thank you for this. More than likely, they will turn their back on you instead and you don't want this, do you?

4. Don't become an island!

There is no shame to have experienced redundancy. Agreed, amongst certain employers there is still an outdated view and unfair suspicion of 'why you' but to a large extent, the mass redundancies over the last few years in both private and public sectors have helped to diminish the previous stigma of redundancy. I have met many people who isolate themselves following their redundancy. Apart from being a potential route to depression, now is the time to 'be out there' talking to people and making things happen, not hiding in your shell.

5. Don't neglect your health

Without your health you have nothing. I've come across many people who have rarely been ill during their employed life but have been blighted by poor health following redundancy, mainly as a result of harbouring many of the negative emotions we looked at earlier in the Chapter. I have also seen examples of people cancelling gym or other sports club memberships or getting into bad eating habits for fear of running out of money.

If you are the sort of person who thrives on a sporty or healthy lifestyle, to stop now will impact in a negative way just at the time you need a boost. Even if you aren't into sport, physical exercise creates endorphins that improve your well being and physical stamina, so at this difficult time, just going for walks and clearing your mind are keys to helping you let go. This point is exemplified by my client, Steve, who had been made redundant and initially neglected himself. Through a combination of exercise and a healthy eating regime, he lost over 2 stones and felt much better about himself and ready to go out and meet people.

6. Don't turn down people's help

If people you value and trust, and other people who have a genuine desire to help you, are offering to help, take it, even if it means 'eating humble pie'. You may never get the offer again and you don't want to regret this, do you?

7. Don't join the negative brigade

It is all too easy to wallow in your own self pity and seek refuge with others in the same situation. This will only bring you further down and prolong your ability to let go. This is not the 'support group' you want or need right now or ever for that matter, is it?

8. Don't spend your life on the internet

You have much work to do before you can even start to think about your next job, especially if you are planning a career change. You will soon come to realise, by reading this book, that there is little or no benefit to spending hours of your time job searching on the internet. This is all too easy but it is time that you can use far more productively working your way through the 6 steps of the Cycle process and the exercises in this book.

9. Don't try to short cut the process and work on your CV yet!

The biggest mistake you can make at this stage is to try to circumnavigate the process, thinking that you will be smart and save time. I have seen this happen with so many people. Unfortunately it rarely works and **the reality is more haste = less speed!**

You don't want to waste time firing out your CV to the world until you have decided what you want to do and have done the work to ensure that your CV is targeted and focused and you have a clear sense of purpose, do you? You will then hit the target and avoid all the frustration that this typical 'scattergun' approach fails to achieve. For example, at one point I was applying for jobs simply in order to feel productive. However, it was a fruitless exercise. I may have been firing lots of bullets, but nothing hit the target. I have worked with many clients who come to me for help at this point of frustration, which is hardly surprising, is it?

Also, don't be influenced by other people who ask whether you have any 'irons in the fire'. Following the process means less haste but ultimately more speed, as your focus will be where it matters. Alternatively, you may be working through the process and thinking you want to start your own business, in which case you are unlikely to need a CV in the traditional sense at all. You may need to focus on other aspects such as your online profile on LinkedIn, which we will revisit in Chapter four.

10. Don't procrastinate

Learn to be proactive and to take control of your career. The worst scenario is to suddenly spring into life only when you become desperate, as I have seen many people do. This is a recipe for disaster. By following the process and doing the exercises in this book you will keep focused.

11. Don't think you already know it all

Even if this is not your first experience of redundancy, your thoughts and feelings might be very different this time round. Also, the world of work has moved on and there are so many new possibilities and opportunities which may not have been available to you previously. Most importantly, you won't have had the benefit of my Career Navigation Cycle process to guide you before. This may help you arrive at completely different conclusions about what you might want to do next, so you could end up taking a very different direction.

12. Don't take the first job offer that comes along

So many people make this mistake because you feel flattered, relieved or because you feel you have got one up on your colleagues. Unless you have an immediate financial need and cannot wait to get round the complete Cycle, I would urge caution, as you could be jumping from the 'frying pan into the fire'. Follow the process and you will get the job or work **you** want!

Perception Versus Reality

In terms of mindset, one of the biggest roadblocks that people face when looking at career transition is all the limiting beliefs they put in their own way. Henry Ford, the American industrialist and founder of the Ford Motor Company, challenged perception when he said, '*Whether you think you can or you can't you are right*'. In other words, it is you who holds the key, so it is now time to challenge your mindset, as you will often see things that are your perception rather than the reality. It is so much easier to see things and behaviours in other people than we can see in ourselves. How often do you give advice to family, friends or work colleagues about their situations but you can't see the wood for the trees yourself?

Imagine one of your friends is telling you about their redundancy situation. They are thinking about changing their career then hit you with some of these statements:

- I'm not sure I have the experience or the confidence to do that
- I like the sound of the job but I have never worked with the type of technology or systems they use
- There will be more experienced people than me going for the job so there's no point in me applying
- They will think I am over or under qualified
- I am interested in doing something different, but I haven't had an interview in years
- I don't know how or where to start looking for jobs
- My age will go against me
- I don't have the skills or know how to start my own business

Consider how you would address these statements

Will you:

Tell your friend that you feel they are wasting their time and to forget the idea as they are better off doing a similar job to the one they have just lost

Or

Challenge why they are making these statements and give them encouragement that they have far more to offer than they think.

And

Ask them for more information about the job or career they are considering and try to allay their fears?

I'm sure you chose the latter two statements, didn't you? This is exactly the thought process I will be taking you through in this book to help you to reframe your thinking. I have always been a firm believer in having a positive attitude and mindset along with great personal attributes such as; passion, hunger, desire, enthusiasm and drive, which together can win the day against more experienced and qualified competition. This is a key learning point; don't let your negative perceptions stop you from following your passions or dream!

The following case study is without doubt of one of the most extreme examples I have ever come across of someone traumatised by their redundancy, who then made a dramatic and swift career change, having reframed her situation. Her transformation was truly remarkable; from a jabbering wreck at the start of her first session to becoming my quickest ever post redundancy career change success!

Alison's Story

Alison was on an outplacement programme with me and thought 'the end of the world had come as we know it' when I first met her. She was rightly concerned at what the future held as she had a young family and her husband was on a low income. How she made such a dramatic career change from an office based senior Admin role to becoming a Teaching Assistant in her local school, is testimony to the Career Navigation Cycle process and what happens when you reframe your thinking and change your mindset. Her story provides some great learning points and practical tips.

Alison was, clearly suffering from shock, traumatised by her situation and spent much of her first session in floods of tears. She was bitter and angry and needed a safe place to let all her angst out. It was important that she rid herself of this emotional turmoil before we could really start moving forward. If you are feeling this way you must also do likewise.

The reality: When I questioned her about her job and how happy she had been, she admitted she had been quietly looking for other jobs for a while, as she felt stale and bored. However, the location suited her as did her part time hours so she could take her kids to school and organise with other parents for them to be collected. She had also worked with her company for 17 years so didn't really see herself moving anywhere else and she didn't know what other job she could do. As you will come to realise, this is one of the most common 'limiting beliefs' which I will dispel throughout this book. As with many clients I have worked with, the reason Alison was so upset was having the rug pulled from under her, when she least expected it. The way the redundancy was handled, just added insult to injury.

Acceptance

Coaching Alison quickly enabled her to admit her redundancy wasn't a bad thing after all. There were some definite plus points which may also apply to you:

1. She had a great chance to look for new opportunities which she hadn't actively been doing before. Although Alison was frustrated, she had been sitting tight in her comfort zone. Now she had no excuse to not break out and explore doing work she loved!
2. Alison had the benefit of a reasonable redundancy pay off, so the family would be ok financially for a while, which is always reassuring.
3. She had an opportunity to re-evaluate her whole family situation and work-life balance.
4. Re-evaluating their situation proved that if she decided to take a lower paid job with less hours, this would benefit her husband who would be able to do more overtime, which could then increase their overall family income. This was a win win situation.
5. Alison came to realise that she did have some great skills and attributes and was highly marketable, so could now look at a career change with a fresh pair of eyes. She often helped out at her kids' school and maybe this was an opportunity to tap into her passion of working with young children?

Having accepted that her situation was an opportunity rather than a threat, she quickly 'let go' and her progress was amazingly swift. By following steps 1-3 of the Cycle, which you will also do soon, things became clear and she developed a real sense of purpose. Once she rebuilt her confidence and self belief and started to project a positive persona, things started to happen for her and she landed a great role in her daughter's school. This was a multiple 'win' situation. Her daughter thought it was great that Mum was working in her school, her husband got to do more overtime, the Deputy Head could see her potential for future roles and it solved the school run challenge!

Key learning

Within the space of a couple of months Alison had turned her life around. She is living proof that you should never rule yourself out of certain jobs because you don't have the 'right' skills or because you may not have the confidence or self-belief to sell yourself. With the right **mindset**, belief and actions, anything is possible within reason! A negative or bitter mindset will only add to your frustration and things will get worse or seem worse to you. Remember '*You are what you think and feel'*, which we will return to shortly when looking at the Law of Attraction.

Fear And Focus

"The only thing we have to fear is fear itself - nameless, unreasoning, unjustified terror which paralyses needed efforts to convert retreat into advance."

Franklin D Roosevelt - First Inaugural Address, March 4, 1933

What stops most people who experience redundancy, from moving forward is change and stepping out of their comfort zone. Typically fear is the culprit. In this section we will discuss fear; fear of the unknown, fear of failure and even fear of success.

Turning Fear Into Focus

Looking back, I now know that fear of success was one of my biggest fears when I set up my business. It may sound silly but I was fearful that my business might become too big, take over my life and I wouldn't be able to do the things I had left the world of employment for and would lose the freedom that I was longing for. I have come to learn that this was a classic limiting belief as there are always ways to combat such situations and anyway what a great problem to have!

When my business did take off and we got involved with some big projects, I had to reframe as I couldn't do everything myself. I had to let go and really enjoyed the process of recruiting some brilliant associates who ran workshops and 1:1 coaching sessions for me, while I was seeing my own personal clients and developing the business. This was the best thing that could have happened for me and my business and became a win win situation. I was providing some great people with work they loved and many have become personal friends. I now look closely at the client's needs before deciding whether it should be me or one of my team who does the work, so my business is no longer totally dependent on me.

The table below shows two acronyms for FEAR. The left side of the table illustrates how most people's perception of fear is unreal, but the perception stops you from taking action. The right side of the table is fear with reframed thinking, making it something you can tackle head on.

FEAR	*INTO*	FOCUS
F alse	**V**	**F** eeling
E vidence	**V**	**E** xcited
A ppearing	**V**	**A** nd
R eal	**V**	**R** eady

Jane's Story

When I first met Jane she was in a bad place. By her own admission she was a highly confident person, who had always achieved whatever she set out to. She had developed her career to a high executive level in a global plc, was previously full of energy and ideas and always had a sense of purpose. As a result of key changes within the company she was given a new challenge and soon afterwards a new boss. This was not a role she felt comfortable or happy doing as she was not playing to her undoubted strengths. Her new boss had a completely different mindset and values to what she was accustomed to. Jane was also spending an inordinate amount of time travelling and being away from her family, something that she was finding increasingly uncomfortable at a time when her children were coming up to major exams.

For the first time in her career she started to feel very differently about her company and was rapidly losing her confidence, energy and self esteem. As difficult as it was for her, she knew that if she could not get back into a role that she wanted, she had to leave and move on as her situation was becoming untenable.

She could not see herself moving to a competitor and on questioning her, it was clear that she liked the idea of being her own boss and even had a 'patchy' vision for starting her own company. However, her biggest concern and the main reason for contacting me was – *"I don't know how I will survive without the corporate umbrella around me".*

What I discovered through the coaching was that FEAR was at the heart of what was really holding her back. This was all the usual fears e.g. fear of the unknown, fear of failure (something she had never experienced), fear of not being able to reposition or reinvent herself, damage to her personal brand, fear of not being able to earn enough and so on.

Jane was astounded when I told her I had gone through all these self doubts and fears and so do most of my clients. Relating her situation back to the previous exercise, were these perceptions or reality? Jane had proved throughout her career that once she had a goal, real focus, clarity and belief, she was capable of achieving anything, so her thinking was clearly an emotional response and perception rather than reality.

With this is mind, I coached Jane on to how to reframe her fear and turn this into focus, using the two FEAR acronyms. The result was quite remarkable and had an immediate and dramatic impact. As a constant reminder to help her, she made a business card with her new business idea on the front and the two FEAR acronyms on the reverse. We did much work around her values, true marketability and personal brand, all of which you will cover in the next two Chapters. As a result, she regained her confidence, self belief and her sense of purpose. In her words *'The clouds lifted and my dark world turned into a glorious bright future. Don't delay, turn your fear into focus and take charge of your own future doing something you love'.*

She has never looked back and has set up her own consultancy and another business venture which she will develop over time. Although she has been tempted to go back into employment by some lucrative offers, she has stuck to her guns and is being true to herself and her values, facing her fears and winning consultancy contracts on her terms!

✎ *Exercise – Fearful Statements*

I will now share with you this simple way to reframe your fears using two different acronyms for FEAR from the fear into focus table. Here are some examples of 'fearful' statements I often hear from clients together with ways to turn them around. Now you have heard Jane's story, consider carefully what fears may be holding you back and WHY and have a go at turning them into something positive. Understanding WHY you are so fearful is so important, as this is often where you will uncover that, like Jane, your fear is mostly perception rather than reality. Of course we are all fearful of certain things and you might be so of a career change, thinking this might not work for you. However, what if it does? How great would that be? I love the sentiments of enigmatic author and blogger, Seth Godin who encourages people to "dance with fear and opportunity". Maybe this approach will change your views on fear? I hope so.

Fear	Evidence	Focus
I'm too old	Many employers now want younger candidates who have a more up to date skill set and cost less	I have a wide range of business and life skills, a positive attitude and years of experience and can bring real value to a company or a business of my own
I won't come across well at interviews	I have never had a formal interview or haven't had one in years	I need help and support to hone my interview skills, so I can sell myself really effectively – I do have lots to offer
I feel like I have become my job title	I have always done this type of work so don't know anything else	I need to understand what is important to me in a future job or career, identify my talents and transferable skills and establish my true marketability

The Law Of Attraction

To put this Chapter into context, one of the fundamental principles of quantum physics, as told by scientists, is that all life is vibrating energy. Therefore, what energy you put out to the universe is manifested back as a result of your thoughts and feelings. Simply put, if you have a negative mindset, are feeling bad about yourself, have self doubts about your abilities, job or career prospects and you focus on what you don't want in life, then this is what will manifest itself back to you and you won't get the promotion or job you want and your negativity will come back to haunt you. Think like the victim, behave like one and you will become the victim.

Conversely, positive energy will attract the same. Positive people radiate energy to those around them, often lighting up their own and others' lives, resulting in positive outcomes. If you have a positive mindset and you are always focusing on what you do want in life, believe in yourself and your ability to make things happen, this is what will manifest for you in the areas of life that you focus on. I'm sure you would rather help the positive person who fuels you with positive energy, than the negative person who drains you, wouldn't you? We will be revisiting this Law and other important laws of success and achievement later in the book.

Michael's Wakeup Call!

A wonderful example which encompasses much of what we have covered in this Chapter; letting go and looking forward, the Law of Attraction, reframing, turning fear into focus, changing mindset and the power of language was with a client who attended an outplacement workshop I ran for a well known transport company a few years ago.

I had explained the Career Navigation Cycle process, the importance of letting go and looking forward and how positive mindset and what you say, how you say it and to whom can influence your outcomes, when in walked Michael about half an hour late. He slumped in his seat, without any apology and started banging on about 'redundancy this and redundancy that' and how badly the company was treating him, how it was getting him down etc, etc. He must have used the dreaded 'R' word a dozen times in the space of a minute. He was bemused by the fact many of his colleagues in the room were laughing heartily. I politely explained that if he had been on time he would know why his colleagues were laughing. He needed to be aware that going on about his redundancy and being negative about the company would not be helpful to his cause. I added that the workshop would focus only on how to be positive and that despite his beliefs, it was not the company's fault that these redundancies had to be made. It was well known these were as a result of external factors completely outside of their control. At least the company was investing considerable time and money providing outplacement support to him and his colleagues, something that not all companies feel obliged to do.

When I met Michael a couple of weeks later for a follow up in a 1:1 session, I shall never forget his opening welcome... '*Steve you will never believe what happened to me following the workshop*'. Michael went on to share that he had not realised the extent of his negative feelings as a result of the impending redundancy. The reaction of his colleagues and my response was a 'wakeup call' and he had taken on board how he needed to change his mindset and work at becoming positive when meeting people, even family and friends and in informal situations.

It transpired that he met a contact for a beer and was discussing his situation and *"how he was going through career transition and exploring new opportunities"*.

He explained it was unlikely he would get similar work in his field, as it was a very specialist type of engineering. He was also not getting any younger and didn't want to take on anything too physical again. He told his friend that he'd done some teaching earlier in his career and was wondering if he could share his wealth of knowledge and experience in a teaching capacity at a college, to benefit engineers of the future. His friend was so impressed by this positive thinking that he immediately said he would be happy to introduce Michael to a contact at a local college. The rest is history and he was at the point of being offered a teaching position when I met him for his final outplacement session.

This was another remarkable shift of mindset, which resulted in one of the quickest success stories I can remember, especially for someone the 'wrong side of fifty'. Most importantly, Michael made a specific point of telling me his success would never have happened if he had maintained his negative mindset.

Build Your Confidence And Rebuild Your Career

Understanding and managing your emotions during your career transition is key to your success. How well you do this, coupled with your attitude and approach to all the other aspects we have covered, will have a significant impact on how quickly you make your successful career transition.

There is a direct correlation between your confidence and what happens when you start to get back on the career ladder or start work of any sort again. Understanding this is very powerful and helps to shape your thinking about what will make the difference to keeping you moving towards your end goal. Your confidence and how you are feeling about yourself and your situation will project very clearly through your body language, tone of voice, energy levels, how you communicate, as with Michael. So, do yourself a favour and take heed of his example.

Summary

- Your past does not equal nor does it dictate your future
- Consider your PERSPECTIVE
- It **is** time for change
- Follow the Do's to manage the 'emotional roller coaster'
- Look at your personal development as a lifelong investment in your growth
- Your mindset really does matter
- You are a work in progress and '*between jobs, exploring new opportunities*'
- Challenge your perceptions – are they real?
- You do have opportunity and CHOICE
- Learn to control your inner dialogue and self talk
- Turn your FEAR into Focus
- Let your positive thoughts and feelings attract what you want
- Build your confidence to grow your career

- Get the right support networks around you
- The Career Navigation Cycle process works – believe in it and take it step by step
- Acknowledge and celebrate your 'small wins'

Congratulations! You are now ready to move to the next step of the cycle: **Re-evaluate**

CHAPTER 2

It's Time To Re-evaluate – Step 2

"You spend more waking hours at work than in any other activity. Life is too short, so why be unhappy? Take the leap of faith and do what you love."

In this Chapter, we will explore Step 2 of the Cycle, which is key to the career transition process. Reflection, review and the output from challenging your thinking are the foundation you will build from. It is something you have probably rarely, if ever, done in any meaningful way. My experience is that most people view their careers and life as separate entities. It's when you start to re-evaluate that you realise your career and life are inextricably linked and you can lead a more fulfilling life by getting the balance right. The 'soul searching' exercises in this Chapter will help you with this re-evaluation. If you have not been in a job or career you love, then now is also the time to change your thinking and beliefs, so that your work becomes a key part of your life fulfilment.

Integral to this process is developing a good understanding of:

- What change **really means** to you
- What is important to you in your career and life and **why**
- The Importance of your Values and Needs
- How your financial situation can reshape your thinking
- Your vision of success

Many people want to start sending out CVs at this point, but as I have previously said, there is much work that needs to be done before you do that. Please do not underestimate the importance and the immense benefit of this re-evaluation stage. There will be a number of exercises to help you re-evaluate in a focused way. These will underpin much of your thinking and decision making as you move round the Cycle both now and for the rest of your career.

Navigate Your Way To A Brighter Future Toolkit

To help you work your way through the exercises, especially if you prefer not to write directly in the book, I have provided many additional resources, including bonus extras not featured in the book, on my website. These tools will add value to the book and are geared to help you work towards achieving your successful career transition or change. The toolkit contains:

- Free electronic worksheets for many of the key exercises in the book
- Free MP3 download -The first 30 minutes of my 'I Want A Career Change' 4CD/MP3 audio book set
- Free downloadable PDF with 5 pages of my Top Career Change Tips

You can download this toolkit of resources by registering at:

http://www.stevepreston thecareercatalyst.com

For some of the exercises, you may want to set up your own spreadsheets, Word (or similar) tables.

Health Warning...

With all of the exercises and key questions in this Chapter and the rest of the book, it is important that you are totally honest with yourself. There is no point in answering in any way other than being true to yourself, as this is the only way you will get authentic output that will enable you to follow through with the required positive action to achieve the outcomes you want.

All Change!

In this Chapter are some wonderful examples of clients and different people I have met who have had major 'eureka moments' when re-evaluating their careers and life situations. Moments which have prompted them to take drastic remedial action to transform their lives. By reading this book and working through the key exercises in this Chapter, you can plan your journey round the Cycle and be proactive too! First we will look at what will need to change in your career and life and most importantly **why**. This will set the scene before we explore what happens if you don't change and conversely from a positive mindset, what happens if you do.

What Needs To Change & WHY?

To get your career transition journey really moving, it is important to put some stakes in the ground to establish your current situation and find out where you are in various key aspects of your **career and life**. This will then help you to re-evaluate where you want to be and most importantly **why** and to prioritise what you want to address.

I often find that clients want to know 'what job or career they could change to or how they could change job or career' at this early stage. My answer is always the same i.e. "*The* ***what*** *and* ***how*** *will come if you trust, believe and follow the career navigation cycle process*". At this stage the most important aspect is **why** you want to change. The **why** is your purpose and if your **why** is strong enough, this will be your call to action and **what** you do and **how** you achieve your change will follow. Understanding **why** and your purpose will help you to take control of your career and 'become the architect of your own future'.

What Happens If You Don't Change?

Revisit the questions in the Introduction on *'How do you feel about your career'.* If you have never been fulfilled in your work, consider this excellent point which has been used by many famous thought leaders along the lines of *"If you always do what you've always done you will always get what you always got".* This surely sums up perfectly what happens if you don't change, doesn't it?

We have already looked at the importance of changing and moving with the times in Chapter one. Despite your redundancy, the longer you have been in a job, industry or particular sector, the harder making the break is likely to be. You may be afraid of making changes, but not changing will have far worse consequences, if you don't want *"what you always got".* Also, the longer you leave your decision to change, the more frustrated you will become and this will impact on your life and those around you, especially your nearest and dearest at just the time you want their empathy and support.

I'm sure you don't want any of these statements to be what becomes of you following your redundancy, do you?

- You never realise your true potential
- You constantly wonder 'what if'
- You become ever more frustrated and unhappy
- You settle for a life of compromise
- You never challenge yourself
- You accept your work is a means to an end
- You become a 'wage slave'

The reality is that when you are unhappy in your work it can have many repercussions with the most severe affecting:

- Your health
- Your relationships
- Your social life
- Your outlook on life

What Happens If You Do Change?

Let's now look at the positive things that can happen when you do make changes, as the following case study illustrates. It's a wonderful example of accepting that change must happen, taking control of your career and taking positive action by investing in yourself and your future.

Sam's Story

A few years ago, I ran my '*Navigate the Way to a Brighter Future*' seminar at the 'One Life Live' exhibition at Olympia in London. Like this book, the seminar, was about how to make a successful career transition or change, with the emphasis on '*Winning Through Redundancy*'. We had an audience of around two hundred people with some people dropping by our stand afterwards to see us and chat. Sam told us how much she had enjoyed the seminar and asked for more information about our career development programmes. She was on the phone to me first thing the next morning asking me if I minded that she had phoned me before I got round to calling her. Goodness me if only all potential clients were that proactive!

She cut to the chase quickly telling me that a comment I made in the seminar had been going round in her head all weekend. I had said, rather tongue in cheek, something along the lines of "*As much as we like seeing you at the exhibition, we don't want to see you again next year, unless it is to share your success.*" This had resonated strongly with Sam as, in her own words, "*If I come back again next year and nothing has changed, I will have failed!*"

Sam was definitely at a career crossroads. She had spent twenty years developing her career with a major plc. She had a good middle management role but by her own admission had lost her way and she no longer shared the values and ethos of the company, which had changed radically. My warning was her call to action and despite her difficult financial situation, she decided it was time to move on and invest in herself and her career for the first time in her life. This begs the question of how few people ever invest in themselves. You may spend money sending your kids to university or have a portfolio of financial investments but you are in the minority if you have ever invested in your own career and personal development. When the benefits can be so significant and life changing, this is crazy, isn't it?

From a standing start, Sam worked her way through my Breakthrough Career Development programme, round the entire Career Navigation Cycle and made a career change in less than three months! Her turning point was the realisation that it was time for her to make changes in her life and take positive action, rather than procrastinating as she had been doing for years. I was so impressed with Sam, especially for her natural coaching and training skills, which we discovered through the coaching. With her enthusiasm, energy and determination, I felt she would make a great coach and trainer herself, which is exactly what happened, as she became one of my associates and a key part of my team. In no time at all she was getting rave reviews from her clients, gained a coaching qualification with the result that her self confidence soared and she was fulfilled!

As I discussed in Chapter one, you can resist change or you can see it as an opportunity. In this Chapter, you will find that change is also a chance to re-evaluate yourself and your life to see if you want to do things differently and reap the rewards, just as Sam did. There are a number of ways of identifying the areas of your life you want to change, which we will explore. As with Sam, the best results come once you accept you must change. You can then take control of your **life and career** to take the positive action to become the architect of your own future. Your next step:

Stock Take

What Is Important To You In Your Career & Life & WHY

In our fast moving world and lives, most people rarely stop and reflect. Instead they tend to stumble through life. Does this sound familiar? Most importantly, following your redundancy, you now have a great opportunity to take stock, put some new stakes in the ground and re-evaluate some key areas of your life. You may even decide to take some time out at this stage, but consider carefully the implications of this which we will look at shortly.

What better time than now to start focusing on getting your life and career into balance and working towards finding a job, career or work you love and creating the life you want? This leads nicely into our first main exercise, *'The Wheel of Life'*. This exercise will help you take a holistic view of your life to establish how balanced your life is and focus your energy on the key areas you wish to improve moving forward. This is an excellent way to kick start your re-evaluation process. The next section will guide you through how to use the exercise for maximum benefit.

✎ *Exercise - The Wheel of Life: Are You Happy With Your Life & Is It In Balance?*

The Wheel of Life is used in many coaching situations because it is an excellent foundation to build on, when looking at making changes in your life. Experiencing redundancy is undoubtedly such a time, so this is a great start point for your re-evaluation of your career and life. You will find other examples of the Wheel of Life. I have adapted this version based on many years of experience working with different types of clients to include what I believe to be the most relevant categories for people in career transition. The exercise may trigger thinking around similar categories you also wish to focus on, which is fine. Otherwise, just work and focus on the categories I have listed.

The Wheel of Life: How balanced is my life?

The Wheel of Life has 8 categories	My Score
Fun - Happiness, Hobbies, Leisure	
Relationship - Current or Future Life Partner	
Career - Job satisfaction, Career path	
Family - Children, Parents, Relatives	
Social - Friends, Sport, Activities	
Health - Exercise, Diet, Well-Being	
Financial - Savings, Investments	
Creative - Self-space, Personal Growth, Spiritual, Artistic	

- Assign a number from 1 to 10 next to each category. Write 1 in the second column if you are very unsatisfied in this area and up to 10 if you are totally satisfied.
- Look at the picture of the circle on the next page. Thinking of the outside of the circle as 10 and the centre as 1, draw a line in each segment to represent your score. You can see a completed example at the bottom of the next page
- Join up the lines between each segment. This represents the balance in your life!
- Look at your scores - What are the 2 lowest scores?
- What are the 2 areas that you would most like to move forward?
- Moving forward:

How would you feel if you could significantly move forward in these 2 areas?

1. ....

2. ....

Action - What could you do now to start moving forward in these areas?

1. ....

2. ....

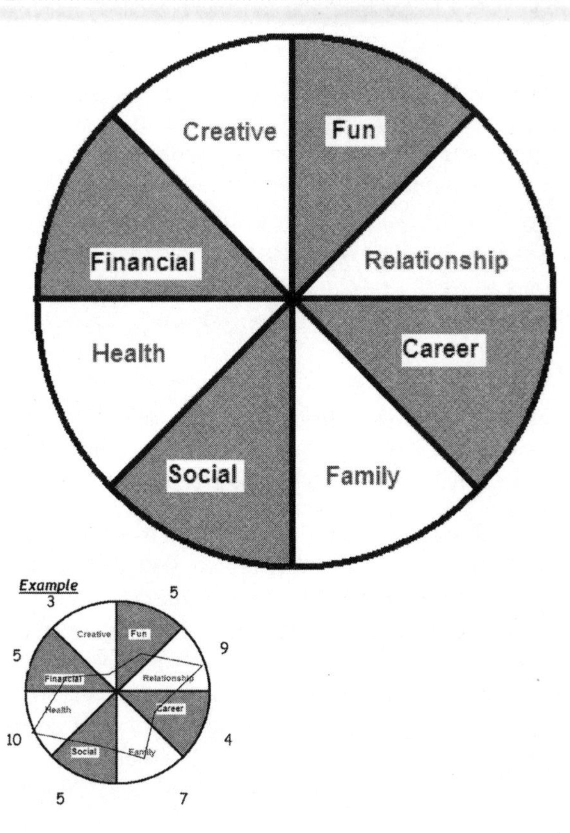

How does your Wheel look?

I can guarantee it is unlikely your wheel of life will be a complete circle, unless the circle has mid to low scores on each segment. The majority of people have a wheel somewhat similar to what you might see on the Flintstones, so don't worry if this is how yours looks as it can only get better from now on. If you, like the majority of my clients, have never seen this exercise previously, you are starting to unravel some brilliant new insights. You may for the first time start to see why you have felt unhappy, prior to your redundancy. Regardless, you can now proactively manage your life to ensure you achieve the right balance for you.

This is just the start of your 'voyage of self discovery.' Importantly, now that you have committed in writing to your focus, you have started making a plan to take action and you are doing something positive about the aspects of your life you want to change. This is a key step in the change process and what gets measured gets done!

How Important Is It To Love Your Job Or The Work You Do?

Confucius, Chinese Teacher, Editor, Politician, and Philosopher (551BC - 479BC) says *"Choose a job you love and you will never work a day in your life".*

What a wonderful fulfilling statement. You may have never considered how important it is to love what you do. Now you are re-evaluating what is important to you in your career and life and **why,** you have reason to do so. Everyone will have a different take on this. However, if you look at people who really do love what they do, most of them are more energised and **they don't even view what they do as work**. Now is your opportunity to work towards achieving this same goal. How good would that feel? Great, I'm sure!

David Attenborough the naturalist and broadcaster, is an extreme but brilliant example. A remarkable man, who at the grand age of eighty six, is still working hard, including all sorts of challenging expeditions for TV shows and enjoying life. Why? Because he is passionate about his work and the Planet! I'm sure you know people like this and they are a joy to be around. This is why I developed my 'mantra', *"You spend more waking hours at work than in any other activity. Life is too short, so why be unhappy? Take the leap of faith and do what you love."*

Some of my clients say *"I don't believe you can actually find work you love. How do people actually end up loving what they do?"* There is no magic wand; there is no 'holy grail'. You need to work through the process, which most people will never do. The answers will eventually evolve from reading this book and following my Career Navigation Cycle process. The following case study highlights vividly what can happen if your life is out of balance and equally what can happen when it is in balance. You now have the opportunity to proactively manage your career to become the architect of your own future and create the life you want. I'm sure you'll agree this sounds appealing, doesn't it?

Boyd Lemon's Story

I came across Boyd on the business social networking site, LinkedIn (I will be making key references to the importance of Social Media and LinkedIn in Chapter four); where I was involved in discussions about the importance of doing what you love. Boyd had made some interesting comments in relation to his life story, so I asked him to provide a short overview for this book. He happily did this and it makes powerful reading:

"As a young man, just out of law school, working for a prestigious Los Angeles law firm, my focus was on doing the best job I could to reach the ultimate achievement - becoming a partner of the law firm. I was married and at the age of 27 became a father, but I relegated my family to second place in my priorities. I was so focused on my work that I ignored my family, particularly my wife's needs, without realizing it. From time to time doubts about whether practicing law, helping the rich to get richer, was what I wanted to be doing, but I pushed those doubts down to the bottom of my consciousness by working hard and using alcohol to numb my consciousness when I wasn't working. Eventually my wife left me. I repeated the same scenario with wives two and three and found myself, at the age of 56, single, still practicing law and abusing alcohol. I began to scratch the surface of my melancholy".

"At 63 I met two young women who helped me break through, both artists, one a dancer, the other a song writer. They became my best friends without any romantic ties. I made plans to retire from the practice of law and one evening I mentioned to the song writer that I would like to write fiction. In two years I wrote about 15 short stories. I loved writing and I finally had found my calling. Doing what you love, probably the single most important thing in life. I didn't understand this for most of my adulthood, but, at least, I finally figured it out."

Boyd focused his first book on his failed marriages and what he learnt about himself through his journey. He published *"Digging Deep: A Writer Uncovers His Marriages* (2011)" and has since published more books, overcome his alcohol problem and is living proof you are never too old to change your career.

Health Warning...

Don't be like Boyd and leave it so late in life to change and do what you love. Why waste so much of your life being unhappy or unfulfilled? Just think what sort of life Boyd might have had if he had listened to his **'inner voice'** about his doubts around his legal career? What he experienced at this early stage of his career was a challenge to his Values and Needs. We will explore the importance of being true to these later in this Chapter.

Fulfilment Or 'Wage Slave'?

Research over the last decade consistently shows that 1 in 2 people are in 'the wrong job' and 2 out of 3 are 'unfulfilled'. This is startling to say the least and such people are effectively 'wage slaves'. We all know people who feel this way about their jobs, who spend their lives moaning and groaning about their company, boss etc. You may have also felt this way before redundancy struck?

Many people inadvertently fall into a job or career, me included. It may not have been part of a master plan but more likely a result of advice you were given, a contact you knew or even family connections getting you started. You may have stayed in the same sector for many years, even if you have changed jobs a few times, perhaps taking on new roles but remaining in your comfort zone and commanding an increasingly good salary. However, there often comes a point when you get stale or the rug is pulled from under you, which then challenges the way you feel about your job or career.

The good news is that, regardless of your situation, you can start to do something positive about your situation now. Life is too short to be forever thinking about 'what if's' so grasp the opportunity and work towards finding the job, career or work you really want and love, so you start looking forward to getting out of bed each day with a real sense of purpose.

The 'Velvet Rut'

A most interesting spin on fulfilment versus 'wage slave' came from a fascinating client, Mary, who coined the phrase the '*Velvet Rut*.' I had never heard of this before but it's a classic description to exemplify how, if you are commanding top packages (she was a City Trader), you get stuck in this awful rut and metaphorical tug of war. On one hand you have a high salary and fantastic bonuses but on the other, you may absolutely hate what you do. The trappings and the lifestyle are what keep you there as it becomes a hard wrench to leave them behind. For many people this is also about ego and 'one-upmanship' over your friends and peers. Only when something happens to suddenly awaken the senses do you realise that this is really not what you want out of life (in most cases it's usually burn out). It makes you sit up, take notice and start to take stock.

I have worked with many people in this situation where it has become blatantly obvious that in most of the areas in their lives they are extremely unhappy and must make changes, but they have to battle against the trappings of 'the velvet rut'. The majority eventually took brave decisions to break out and change their lives. We will come back to Mary later in the Chapter after we look at Values and Needs.

What Does Success Mean To You?

"Success is a journey not a destination"

Ben Sweetland, Author and Psychologist

We have explored how unhappy we can become when stuck in unfulfilling jobs, yet what fulfils us at work and in our lives and to what extent we live to work is so different for each of us. Have you ever really thought about your vision of success? Is it about money and material wealth, travel, a balanced lifestyle, health and happiness or a combination of all these? The Wheel of Life exercise and the Values and Needs exercise, in this Chapter, may also give you some inspiration for your vision of success, so you can start work on your journey.

✎ Exercise – What Is Your Vision Of Success?

You are probably starting to get a picture of many things you don't want out of life but let's now consider what you really **do want** out of life. What does success mean to you in terms of your work and personal life? Your redundancy may have reshaped your thinking around this but it is important that you have a vision of success to aspire to. The Wheel of Life exercise is an excellent start point but the aim here is for you to 'dig deep' and consider what does success mean for you? *What do you see and feel?* Picture this, statement this or do both, whatever works best for you.

To aid your thinking, here are three key questions for you to consider:

1. What do you want to be?

2. What do you want to do?

3. What do you want to have?

These three aspects are key principles in the Law of Attraction and by focusing your thoughts and feelings on your vision, it can help you manifest and attract the right people, work, opportunities etc.

You can do this in a number of ways:

- Draw a picture on a large sheet of paper that represents your vision of success
- Make a collage by cutting out pictures from magazines to build up a picture of what success looks like to you
- Create using an online vision board. There are now many of these excellent resources readily available at no cost or low cost on the web (check out the Useful Resources section in the book)
- Write a short story about your vision or even 'A Successful Day in your Life'

Health Warning...

It is important not to hold back when doing this exercise. You are envisioning the creation of your own wonderful future. This is your vision and therefore nothing is out of bounds, as anything is possible with the right mindset, belief and positive actions, so dream away!

Once you have done this exercise it is worth pinning up your vision board, drawing or story somewhere in your house so that you can see it every day. Taking this approach has worked really well for some of my most successful clients, as the constant reminder of your vision of success will be implanted into your subconscious mind and will spur you on to achieve your dream or goals. Give this exercise your best shot. You can always revisit it as you progress through the book and gain new ideas and inspiration flashes through your mind!

What Gets You Out Of Bed Each Day?

No not that old joke about your alarm clock or Smartphone! Having done some stock taking, you are now starting to gain real insight into what is important to you in your career and life and why. Digging deeper, we now want to consider some of your key motivators and drivers, as this will give you even more powerful information to help you re-evaluate. Let's now look at your must have Values and Needs in your career and life because this will provide some real clues as to:

- Why you want to work
- What really gets you out of bed each day

Understanding Your Values & Needs

"Success goes where your energy flows."

We all have a set of values; they are the things we believe in and hold dear. They often change over time. We are unlikely to have exactly the same values as an adult that we had as a teenager, but we rarely audit or even consider them. We also have a set of needs. These are things that we must have in order to feel motivated and they contribute to our overall sense of wellbeing. Without understanding your values and needs it is almost impossible to find real meaning and fulfilment, which is fundamental when it comes to finding the right work for you. You need to establish:

- What motivates you?

- What drives you?
- What you want to take forward with you in the future?

You rarely consider your Values and Needs until redundancy or a restructure, some other life changing event or the fact that you are so fed up with your job that you walk away and have to start all over again. Values and Needs are things we probably take for granted. In my case it was really brought home to me big time after the death of my Father. At that time I was considering rekindling my executive career. Suddenly this felt hugely insignificant, as there were far more important things in life, not least how on earth my Mother would cope without him, as they had been 'joined at the hip' for over fifty years. I realised that having more flexibility was something I now valued and needed.

When I was working in the corporate world, one of my ambitions was to retire at 55. I thought by then I would have done enough and would want to slow down. I had visions of spending my time doing things I enjoy, like more time to play golf, more time with my wife, taking more holidays and the other things you rarely get the chance to do when you are working full on for an employer. Since doing what I love, in the career coaching world, writing, speaking and running my business, retirement couldn't be further from my mind. I am now past the magic 55 and want to carry on working for as long as I feel I'm enjoying it. My ultimate reward is making a difference to the lives of other people by helping them to transform their careers and lives. There is no better feeling for me and this is what drives me. I guarantee that whatever career plan you've set, once you change career and start doing something you love, your whole perspective will change and how good would that feel?

Let's now assess your own Values and Needs with this simple but effective exercise:

✎ *Exercise - Values And Needs - Getting To Know You*

The table below shows some of the most common or important Values and Needs, which will ultimately help you to consider what you want out of a future job, career or working lifestyle. You will find a challenging online version of this exercise on my website via this link: **http://www.steveprestonthecareercatalyst.com/index.php/component/hikashop/product/cid-33?Itemid=121**

Show **CVN10** in the Coupon box **to save £10**

So, what do you want from a future job or working lifestyle?

Example: if you think *freedom to make my own decisions* is really important, you would tick this in the Essential column. Likewise, if *long term security and stability* is no longer important, as let's face it how can you guarantee this anymore, you would tick the Not Important column and so on.

		Essential	**Desirable**	**Not Important**
AUTONOMY	Freedom to make my own decisions			
	Working autonomously			
	Freedom from organisational rules and constraints			
	Ability to define my own tasks, schedules and procedures			

STABILITY & SECURITY	A clearly mapped out career path			
	Job that requires steady, predictable performance			
	Long term security and stability			
	Working in a stable, well-known organisation			
	Incremental pay and benefits based on length of service			
ENTERPRISE	Creating new organisations, products and services			
	Building my own business			
	Owning something developed from my ideas and efforts			
	Producing things that people associate with me			
	Showing people I can build a fortune			
	Being able to take risks			

SENSE OF PURPOSE	Providing a service to help others			
	Contributing to the wider community			
	Dedication to a particular course			
	Having a job of real value			
	Making a difference in the world			
BALANCED LIFESTYLE	A balanced personal and professional lifestyle			
	Flexible working hours and practices (able to work at home)			
	Relatively low levels of geographical movement			
	Sufficient time for pastimes, holidays and relaxing			

EXPERTISE & CHALLENGE	Developing a specialism to a high level of excellence			
	Being recognised as an expert in the field			
	Ability to use my special skills and talents			
	Solving complex problems			
	Regular challenges to stretch my abilities and skills			
REWARD & RECOGNITION	Having a good standard of living			
	Being recognised for my achievements			
	Having a well paid job			
	Being highly regarded by others			
	Reaching a respected social status			

AUTHORITY & INFLUENCE	Responsibility for making decisions			
	Advancement up the organisational ladder			
	Ability to influence, supervise, lead and control people			
	Contributing to the success of my organisation			
	Accountability for finances and resources			
GENERAL	Variety			
	Physical challenge - you enjoy doing something that is physically demanding			
	Working with others, in a team			
	Contact with people			
	Creativity - thinking up new ideas and ways of doing things			
	Working alone			

GENERAL	Place of work - it is important that you work in the right part of the country for you			
	Competition- you enjoy competing against other people or groups			
	You like working to deadlines			
	Communication - being able to express ideas well in writing and speech			
	Precise work which involves great care and concentration			
	Peace - to have few pressures or uncomfortable demands			
	Artistic - work involving drawing, designing, making music, making models			
	Having close friendships at work			
	Excitement in your work			
	The opportunity to learn new things			

Next Steps

- Taking your **'Essential'** category only, select your **top ten** values and needs
- Now **prioritise these with one being the most important** and **ten the least important**
- The aim is to get a **focused top ten** that you feel is a true representation of what you value and need most from a future job or work
- You can also **map your top ten Values and Needs against your present or most recent jobs** and this will help to explain why you enjoyed some more than others
- You now have powerful information you can use to establish if any jobs you might be considering are right for you, whether you need to rethink or if self employment is an option

What Are Your Values & Needs Telling You?

Are there any surprises?

Look closely, as you may well find clues emerging that you might not have previously considered. Keep an open mind and you never know what opportunities may appear. For example, you may now feel that *contributing to the wider community* is something you would highly value. If so, this could open up a whole new world of thinking around the type of job, organisation, sector or even a business you could start of your own. This is highly individual, so there is no right or wrong. What is important is what feels right for you, looking forward to your *'brighter future'*.

Back to **Mary**, she was a classic example of someone whose Values were completely at odds with both the organisation she worked for and the type of work she was doing. It got so bad that one day she just decided she'd had enough and walked out! Mary was then committed to following her dream - she wanted to be a paramedic. By following the Cycle process, she ultimately achieved her ambition, despite having to overcome many challenges around her fears and limiting beliefs, which you may also have to face at various stages along the way. If Mary did and won through, you can too!

Mary proved that if your Values are at odds with the organisation and what you want to achieve in your life and all the other key strands of your life aren't working, then you must address these particular areas before the consequences are too great. Coincidentally, I have just heard from her, whilst putting the finishing touches to the book. Mary has since relocated, changed her career again, moved into a front line role in a hospital and also got married! Mary has shown what can happen when you get your life in balance, understand your Values and Needs and live your life by them.

How To Work In The Future - Introducing Portfolio Careers

As you can see, when you start to re-evaluate things, it can open up a new world of possibilities. Some of my clients choose to find another job, change careers or set up their own business. Also, many of them have chosen to develop a 'portfolio career'. We will cover portfolio careers again in Chapters three and four in particular, as the appeal for such an approach often increases after you have completed Step 3 of the Cycle (establishing your true marketability) after which you may decide to seriously consider a portfolio career during Step 4 (exploring opportunities).

Essentially, a portfolio career is about changing your mindset from having 'a job' to earning income from a range of skills and activities that help you create the working lifestyle you want. How good does this sound?

These could include:

- A part time employed job and your own business
- Two or three part time jobs, similar or different
- A part time job or your own business and voluntary work
- Regular interim or freelance projects alongside other occasional work (we will cover these options in Chapter five)
- Being your own boss but having different strands to your business or even having different businesses
- A full time employed job and developing your business alongside this

As we go through the book I will give examples of clients and other people I know who have interesting and fulfilling portfolio careers. To whet your appetite let's look at my best mate Don:

Don's Story

Don is a gardener, trainer, career adviser, outplacement consultant, CV writer and a magician! After many years in the rat race, Don took redundancy and decided to work locally and do something he really loved. Don never got the benefit of any outplacement or other career support; instead he discussed his thinking with his wife and with me over a beer in our local pub, which is always a useful refuge for creative thinking!

After doing his survival budget (see next section) Don decided to start up his own gardening business, which was a real passion. Eventually, he developed a portfolio career using a number of other skills and interests. Within a short period of time he added training to the mix (he was a qualified trainer from his previous role) and over time, I networked him into Career Advice & Guidance and the whole Career Development field. Don then added another lifelong interest and passion and turned his love of magic (previously just a hobby) into another income stream.

An amazing day, a few summers ago, Don did gardening in the morning, ran our career transition workshop in the afternoon and finished the day with a magic show for a local society in the evening. What a different way to earn a living by doing all the things you love?

I should point out that Don does not work excessive hours but chooses how and when he works, ensuring he maintains a good work-life balance. Having known Don for many years, I never envisaged him running his own business. I am convinced this was never on his radar until his job was made redundant and he had to re-evaluate his options. Twenty years on, Don is still self employed and has even turned down employed jobs during this period because his portfolio career offers him the choice, variety and flexibility he values most.

Reassess & Rethink Your Finances

Whether you have been out of work for a while, are facing redundancy, considering a career change or if you are planning on starting your own business, then understanding and re-evaluating your finances are of the utmost importance. Let's get started, as by doing this exercise thoroughly it can help you focus your mind and open up new thinking in ways you may not have considered previously.

What Do You Need To Live On?

Pension

If you have had a relatively long career and paid into company pension schemes for a number of years, unless the majority of your pension is held in a public sector scheme, I would highly recommend getting an independent review. When you are in the cut and thrust of daily working life, you may take just a cursory glance at your annual pension statement. Don't assume your pension is working OK for you. Despite thirty years of contributions, my pension was going significantly backwards, due to market conditions and poor investments from the trustees. I contacted a friend, who is an Independent Financial Adviser, and I owe him a huge debt, as he helped to redress my underperforming pension and we now review the performance at least once a year. You don't want to be in the same position as I was, do you? If you are in a company pension scheme and your employer does not provide a pension review as part of your exit, I recommend you take this action yourself, sooner rather than later.

✎ *Exercise - Survival Budget*

Knowing how much you need to earn as against how much you want to or have earned in the past is an invaluable exercise. *Why?* Quite simply, because this becomes the yardstick from which you can work to focus your mind on what might be possible. For example:

You may have had a brilliant career and earned a six figure or 'high' salary but have now had enough of the corporate world or working at an executive level in the public services and have decided that you want to get out of the 'rat race'. It is highly likely you will be earning less when you first make your change, especially if you start up your own business. By doing your sums, you can see very easily how much you need to earn, which is a great start point, don't you think?

For many people, the older you are the less your outgoings become, especially once any children have flown the nest. Therefore, if you've had a good or long career your survival budget can often be a pleasant surprise. For younger people, if you have a high mortgage or family overheads, it could be harder to make that change into work you would really love to do. You may need to make some major sacrifices or compromises, especially if you cannot afford to be out of work for any length of time. This doesn't mean to say you cannot achieve your desired goal for a career change but you may need to consider whether this becomes a medium or longer term goal instead or work towards this alongside another job. Ultimately, if you are seeking fulfilment, you don't want to let your financial situation hold you back, as I'm sure you don't want to be thinking '*what if*', for years to come do you?

Note: This is a personal survival budget not a business one. If you decide to start up your own business you will need to add in various start up and running costs, which you will need to research. We will review self employment and starting a business in more detail in Chapter five.

Complete the following table of income and outgoings. Your total survival budget equals your income minus your outgoings.

Monthly income		**Monthly outgoings**	
Partner salary/ income.		Mortgage or rent.	
Other income e.g. rent from working children.		House – insurances plus general maintenances.	
Interest from savings.		Car/s - mot, tax, insurance plus running costs including petrol.	
Dividends from shares and other investments.		Utilities – electric, gas, phone, mobile, broadband, TV etc.	
Tax credits if applicable.		Food – typical weekly shop.	
Child Benefit.		Holidays – budget for what you typically spend.	
Pension (if able to draw some/all).		Leisure – watching and playing sport, gym membership, hobbies, music, cinema.	
Other income.		Social – Meals out, entertaining, pub.	

Lump sum compromise or redundancy package (if applicable) broken into 12 monthly chunks.		Children – pocket money, schooling, clothes, entertaining, trips, and school holiday clubs. If older then university costs.	
		Clothes for you and your partner.	
		Grooming – hairdressing, make up and accessories.	
		Birthdays, Christmas.	
		Pets – food, insurance, upkeep etc.	
		Subscriptions – magazines, trade publications.	
		Contingencies.	
		Other outgoings:	
Total income		**Total outgoings**	
	Total Survival Budget		

Note: this will be net of tax, so you need to add 20% to 30% on top to allow for this!

Having completed your budget, you can now work out how much you need to earn in order to survive. Here is an example: if your annual income is £30,000 without your salary and your outgoings total £50,000 you will need to earn £20,000 net of tax yourself in order to balance your household outgoings to survive. At the current UK tax band rates this would equate to around £25,000 gross salary or self employed income. Much will depend on what other allowances you are entitled to. To be totally sure you would need to check with HMRC (http://www.hmrc.gov.uk/rates/it.htm) to establish your situation. If you are living outside the UK then you would need to check with your respective government tax department.

Now that you have identified your incomings and outgoings, it is worth working out how long your savings or redundancy pay will last if you aren't working for a while or if you are starting a business from scratch. It will definitely pay you to get some impartial financial advice to review how best to invest either your redundancy money or any inheritance you might be about to receive. This will help you create the life you want now and in the longer term.

Malcolm's Story - Shaking off the shackles of corporate boardroom life

"I was a plc board director who was 'very bored' with big company politics. I had wanted to go it alone for years but lacked the courage. Then one day I was holed up at home with the flu and for once had time to think about my future. I decided that now was the time to be bold and set about calculating all my worldly goods, investments, savings etc.

I determined that if I started my business venture and it didn't work out, I would still be able to support my young family; we would just have to move to a smaller house. This was all the reassurance I needed to take the leap of faith that I had previously not been brave enough to take. I resigned my position 3 days later when I returned to work. That was 13 years ago. Regrets? None - except I should have done it sooner!"

Malcolm's story demonstrates the real benefit of doing your survival budget. It literally provides you with the evidence you need to make your decision. This is what other clients have said over the years, having worked out their survival budgets:

'Maybe I could get a part time job while I develop my business to help pay the bills'

'I can still do the voluntary work I enjoy outside of work as long as I cover my living costs'

'I will get another full time job and develop my business idea at my own pace'

'I don't need to work at the same level again so could consider doing a less stressful job, just working part time and spending more time on my hobbies or developing a portfolio career'

Survival Tips

1. Allow for 'desirables'

- From my own experience and having supported thousands of people through redundancy, it is good to build in 'desirables' as you still need to live.
- This is especially true if you have children who might not understand why all of a sudden they can't do the things they have been used to.
- Also for you, this is an important part of your general well-being and happiness.

2. See where you can make savings

- Use your list of outgoings to help you trim excessive or unnecessary costs to save money.

- Have a close look at your phone, TV and broadband packages, all your insurance policies, gym membership etc to see if you are able to get a better deal, which can then pay for a nice treat at some point.

A number of years ago I had a client who went through his bank statement to see where he could trim his costs. He was shocked to discover how much he spent on CDs and DVDs prior to his redundancy. By his own admission, many were gathering dust on his shelves. He decided to cut these out altogether and saved himself a few hundred pounds a month of unnecessary expense immediately. See what you can trim back that you won't miss or where you can make immediate cost savings.

3. Don't skimp unless you have to

- I have come across many people who go through the survival budget process and decide to cut everything to the bone and as a result don't go out and avoid spending money at all costs!

- Unless your finances are in dire straits, it is important not to 'become an island', as I mentioned in Chapter one.

- Your career transition is a time when you need to meet people to build and develop relationships and new networks. This need not cost you lots of money, just the occasional coffee, beer or glass of wine. However, if you are really strapped, get the other people to pay and make sure you return the favour when you are back on your feet again.

4. Build in contingencies

- Always allow for the unexpected e.g. repairs to your car, work on the house or electrical items needing replacement.

5. Worst case scenario

- How long will your money last and what would happen if your money ran out?
- What would your options be? For example:
    - You could look for temporary work or an interim contract rather than a new full time role for immediacy of work.
    - Alternatively, if you have a partner who is not working would it be more beneficial for them to find work if they can command a higher salary and you swap household roles? I have a number of clients who have done this.
- If you decide to start a business, it may be helpful for your partner to secure a better paid job or even part time work whilst you are getting established to cover your bills.

6. Taking remedial action

- If your situation is such that your money will soon run out, there is still positive action you can take, to salvage your situation, whilst you decide what your next step will be.
- I know a number of people, who decided to rent out a spare room in their house for a period of time to give them breathing space, while they made their career transition, set up a business or were growing their business to the next level. This can often work

well to give you time while you get back on your feet again. Also, if you live alone, this can help to offset the isolation.

- In extreme cases, where you need to take drastic action in order to fund a business or you wish to have an easier life in the twilight years of your career, you always have the option to downsize your property to free up some cash.

If you follow through with the principles and the guidelines in this book, you stand a much better chance of not needing to take such radical action. However, being aware of the options will focus your mind on the final deadline by which you need to achieve your end goal and successful career transition.

7. Continue the discipline

- Once you have developed your survival budget, this is an excellent discipline to continue. It becomes a constantly evolving project as and when your circumstances change e.g. kids leaving home, going to university, your partner changing jobs, you getting a better or lesser paid job, moving house or your business really taking off. You now have a readymade tool to help you budget.

What would you be reluctant to give up?

Both my wife and I have a background in the travel industry, so holidays have always been important to us and an integral part of our life and budget. When I took redundancy, we still had holidays but toned them down until I was earning well again. Now our children are independent, we only need to budget for the two of us, but our aim is to have a break of some kind every 4 months to keep us fresh and always have something to look forward to. Holidays are a big chunk of our annual survival budget but equally a key part of our 'life plan', taking priority over other desirables.

How has your survival budget affected your thinking?

Having completed this exercise you may have identified areas where you can start saving or you have found you don't need to earn as much as you thought. This can be extremely liberating, which can open up completely new thinking, as was the case for me. When I realised how much I needed to earn versus what I had been earning, I felt confident that I would be able to generate this income from running my own business, given all the skills, attributes and knowledge I had developed over the years. Although I did not know what I wanted to do at this stage, it was hugely reassuring to know I would only need to earn around half of my previous salary, so starting a business suddenly felt very achievable. What would a similar scenario mean for you?

Is It Time For A Break?

Having done your financial evaluation, you may decide you have the money and inclination to take advantage of your downtime to travel or for other projects you have never had the time for when fully employed. You may want to take the gap year you never had, maybe doing some long term volunteering for a worthwhile cause to rejuvenate you and provide fulfilment whilst developing new skills? Consider - you may never get a better opportunity than now.

Health Warning...

For some people it is a good thing to take a break to stock take. However, such a decision needs careful consideration. I was given the advice to *'take the summer off and get my head straight'* by my outplacement consultant. However, what I learnt during my transition and have seen many times since with clients is, the longer the break the harder it is for you to 'get back in the saddle'. Three months can easily become six months and before you know it a year goes by and you have not moved any further forward. Equally, it can become easy to fill your days with so many projects that you wonder when you ever had time to work!

I had one client who said *"he had enjoyed himself so much for the past year as it was the first time he had spent quality time with his young family but now needed to take some positive action as the money was running out!"* He was fortunate that he got support at just the right time when he was in the right mindset to get back into work mode. He was receptive to what he needed to do to be successful, got focused, proactive and landed a good job quickly. For many other people the reality can be very different. The longer you are out of work, the more likely it is that you will fill your days with other distractions such as home projects or unproductive job searching, for the sake of it. This is when desperation can creep in and you don't want to be in this situation, do you?

My advice: if you feel the time is right for you to take a break because you have specific goals or aspirations then fantastic. However, unless you have substantial finances, it pays to begin the job search, as it is all too easy to lose your work ethic. Also, if you are planning to get back into employment, the reality is, it is always easier to do so when you have only had a short break, as being out of work for many months often puts the seed of doubt in an employer's mind.

Paul's Story

An excellent example which helps to encapsulate much of the learning from this Chapter is Paul, a top strategic IT Consultant, who told me his story:

"My moment of truth came to me when I was 30,000 feet in the air. I was heading across the Atlantic to America in mid July having travelled 60,000 air miles that year. I had a loving partner and two boys now entering their teenage years. It dawned on me that I was literally travelling the wrong way (in so many ways). My career progression was in control of me rather than the other way around. At risk was the loss of a loving family, which felt unacceptable. I put away my ego and fear.

The solution was radical. With no plans for the future I resigned and was gone within a month. I took the family on holiday for the summer and started to build relationships with the people that really mattered to me. My boss thought me completely mad! However six months later I had set up a consultancy and won contracts. I was earning more than when I had travelled the world as a senior employee. I was in control of my career and never looked back. Today I have what many people spend most of their lives looking for: CHOICE.

I can work on things that I find motivating; it just so happens that I also make good money and every day is interesting. My best friends are my family and I go to sleep each night contented and thank my god for giving me a good kicking at 30,000 feet! One year after I had resigned I heard that 8,000 jobs were lost at the company I had worked for, including the boss who thought me mad. In fact, my function was completely cut, so where would I be now?"

What can we learn from Pauls' story?

The majority of these learning points can be found in the Summary below. Another key point is, if you have been neglecting your partner or family, this could be a great time to bring you closer by taking a lengthy break. It will also give you some breathing space to re-evaluate your career and life. If you do decide to start your own business, the break will be viewed by potential clients as doing research, business planning and getting 'your ducks in a row'.

Summary

I trust that some of the inspiring stories in this Chapter will make you sit up, want to re-evaluate and to take control of your career to 'become the architect of your own future' to find work you love! Also:

- You are never too old to change
- Doing what you love will lead to fulfilment in your work and life
- Discover how balanced and how happy you are with your life
- Establish what needs to change and ***Why*** and start work on this now
- Do you want to be a 'wage slave' or break free and do what you love?

- Reassess your finances to understand how much you need to earn to reframe your thinking
- Put the survival tips into practise and continue the disciplines
- A lengthy break is good but only if you have the money and a specific goal
- You may not want a traditional job any longer, if so an option is to consider a portfolio career
- Understand the importance of your Values and Needs and what gets you out of bed each day
- What is your vision of success? Dream it, feel it, see it, display it so you can make it happen
- Think about what happens if you don't change and imagine how you will feel if you do!

Congratulations! You are now ready to move to the next stage of the cycle: **Establishing your true marketability.**

CHAPTER 3

Establishing Your True Marketability – Step 3

"When who you are aligns with what you do you will achieve extraordinary results."

Laura Berman Fortang - Renowned Speaker, Author & Life Coach

What is your true marketability, you might be thinking? I get asked this question all the time. How does this differ from your marketability? The secret lies in Laura Berman Fortang's fantastic quote. Establishing your *'true marketability'* is about **getting to know yourself, understanding who you are and what you have to offer the world.** This is so much more than establishing and marketing your transferable skills. This step is where you really bring yourself to life by exploring and uncovering your 'complete personal package', which we will look at shortly. The insight you gain will move you from '*who am I*' to revelations about yourself that you may never have considered were possible. This is why Step 3 is at the heart of the Cycle and is an integral part of your career transition journey to help you move forward with renewed confidence, self belief and motivation.

As with Step 2, it is unlikely you will have done the type of in-depth analysis and 'soul searching' we will cover in Step 3. 'Digging deep' will make the process exciting and motivational with the exercises helping to unlock your potential, uncover hidden talents and open up new thinking about what opportunities might be possible for you in your career moving forward. I tell all my clients that Step 2 and Step 3 plus adopting the right mindset are what really make the difference to winning through redundancy. How good will it feel to know you can add powerful content to your CV, be more confident in interviews and sell yourself in a much more compelling and meaningful way? Equally, that you really do have the skills and potential to run your own business if you desire. Great, I'm sure.

In this Chapter we will explore:

- Understanding your true marketability so you can make this work for you

- Why it is important to be true to yourself and work from 'the inside out'
- Why you still have much work to do before sending out your CV
- Your complete package and what the 'bigger picture' entails
- Inspiring case studies of people who have used their true marketability to great effect
- Whether Personality Profiling may or may not help you
- Your Personal Brand and the importance of this to your career moving forward

Marketability

Why Is It So Important To Understand Your True Marketability?

First and foremost, you are probably like most people who greatly undersell and under value themselves and find it difficult to 'blow your own trumpet'. Unfortunately, the reality is that if you don't tell people how good you are, it is unlikely anyone else will. So, by understanding who you are and what you have to offer, this will help you:

- Get a much better handle on what might be possible for you to consider moving forward
- Determine whether you wish to be employed or self employed
- If you wish to be employed this key insight will help you rewrite your CV to be targeted, focused and sell you in the best light

- If you decide on self employment, consider options for your business venture
- Determine whether a portfolio career is right for you as a result of your range of skills, talents, interests and passions
- Bring yourself to life so it will become easier to explain who you are and what you have to offer when meeting people informally or selling yourself in networking situations
- Achieve a big boost to your confidence and self esteem by realizing you have so much more to offer than you thought
- Move forward to the upward swing of the 'emotional roller coaster'
- To help you take control of interviews, if you learn how to use your newly gained knowledge effectively (see Julie and Sarah's case studies)

Working 'Inside Out' - Be True To Yourself And Life Will Be True To You

If you want to establish your '**true** marketability' you must be totally honest with yourself. Your thoughts must come from your heart. The majority of the exercises in this book will challenge you to think from 'your inside out'. This means you will be using your heart more than your head. The fundamental difference means that your responses are far more likely to represent the authentic you.

Working on 'an authentic you' will have the greatest impact on finding a job, career or work you love and leading a fulfilling lifestyle. Sometimes you might cloud the issue by taking shortcuts and trying to let your head control your heart. We will revisit this point when we look at Personality Profiling, one area where the head does take control.

Top tips for working through the exercises to be true to yourself

- Accept that getting to know your true self and what you have to offer, is at the heart of the Career Navigation Cycle hence don't be tempted to take short cuts
- Do not underestimate the amount of work, time, effort and mental energy you will need to spend on this crucial stage of the process
- Be patient and stick with the process as "you reap what you sow", as the saying goes
- You may find it easier and more rewarding to work in 'bite size chunks' so you can see gradual results from your efforts

Showcasing Yourself

CV = 'Curriculum Vitae' OR 'CircumVenting' The Process?

Consider this scenario:

You are facing redundancy or have just left your employer. You believe you need to look for another job so you immediately dust off your CV, consider updating it, adding relevant new information, then fire it out to as many companies, organisations, agencies and job boards as possible. Does this sound familiar? **STOP** and ask yourself this key question: Is this the best use of your time and course of action at this early stage? By taking this approach you will have joined the majority of job seekers blazing the same path following redundancy. Do you want to be part of the sheep mindset or do you want to become the architect of your own future and take control of your life and career? The latter I'm sure sounds more appealing, doesn't it?

Interestingly, many outplacement and career management consultancies will have you following exactly this route because it is arguably the 'easy' option, as in theory you can get cracking on your CV straight away. However, by taking this route and circumnavigating all the time consuming but crucial 'soul searching', you could easily end up 'out of the frying pan and into the fire' and I'm sure you don't want that, do you?

What Is Wrong With This Approach, I Hear You Say?

I know to my own cost and working with many clients over the last decade, that taking this approach at this early stage is often the biggest mistake that many job seekers inadvertently make. Why? Because there is much work to be done before updating and rewriting your CV and blasting it out to 'the universe'. Taking this approach is unlikely to get you on the interview 'YES' pile, unless you have first established and understood your true marketability. Without having done this work and taken this key step in the Career Navigation Cycle process, you are essentially 'putting the cart before the horse'.

In my experience, at this early stage of the redundancy process, unless you have already had the foresight or support to consider who you are and what you have to offer before you left your employer (in which case brilliantly well done but you are a rare breed), your CV is unlikely to be targeted, focused or sell you in the best light. Also, you really need to take a step back, follow the steps highlighted in Chapters one and two and then utilize all the nuggets in this Chapter, if you want to create maximum impact with your CV. Your CV may even become virtually redundant, if you decide to pursue other options such as self employment or a portfolio career. The unfortunate reality is that most people who have not experienced redundancy before (and even some who have) will automatically go into panic mode at this difficult stage. You feel obligated to be doing something positive towards finding your next job and therefore follow what seems to be the most obvious route to market. I can assure you the reality is very different.

Consider this scenario:

Imagine two CV's landing on an employer or recruiter's desk, - the first one is purely skills focused and the second one really brings the person to life in a very positive and powerful way so that their personality, work ethic, career objectives, achievements and energy leap off the page. Unless the skill level is the only prerequisite for the job, who are you going to invite to interview? The second one, I'm sure.

Developing an in depth self awareness of who you are and what you have to offer is essential for effective self marketing and developing your career. This provides focus and clarity to ensure that you are applying for the right jobs, your applications are targeted and you sell yourself in the best light on your CV and also in any networking or interview situations.

Health Warning...

Please resist the temptation to shortcut the Career Navigation Cycle process as I can guarantee that 'more haste will become less speed'! Whilst you might feel you are doing something positive (as the firing out of your CV to the universe may feel cathartic), this is what I call taking a classic 'scattergun' approach, where you fire lots of bullets but few, if any, will hit the target.

How Circumnavigating The Process Can Impact At Interviews

If you should get called to an interview at this stage, you might be excited. However, unless this is as a result of some networking or from a previously known contact, this could be a result of more luck than judgement. As you won't have got to grips with who you are and what you have to offer and understand your true marketability yet, you are highly unlikely to sound compelling and give the best account of yourself at interview. Moreover, you will be like the majority of people (regardless of their level) who dramatically undersell themselves and lack confidence at the time you need it the most. In addition, you won't have worked through fully what sort of job or career is right for you. Therefore, even if you are offered the job, you risk the danger of yet another example of jumping 'out of the frying pan and into the fire', which you don't want, do you?

If you keep getting invited to interviews before you have completed the work around your true marketability, you don't sell yourself effectively and are not offered the job. If this trend continues you actually start to dread, rather than desire, being invited to interviews. You can go into a downward spiral, not wanting to apply for jobs for fear of rejection. This is when your motivation, confidence and self esteem can be shot to pieces, as we covered in Chapter 1 and it can become a vicious circle. This is not what you want is it, at this delicate stage of your career transition process, just when you should be looking forward to starting on a positive upswing on your 'emotional roller coaster ride'?

Your 'Package'

Skills Are Important But They Are Only Part Of The Picture

Most career books and career consultancies highlight the importance of knowing your skills and especially transferable skills, when it comes to looking at a new job or career. This is absolutely right as of course these are always important. However, skills are only part of what you have to offer. Understanding the concept of '*true marketability*' as your 'complete package', 'the whole you' and what you have to offer, is a powerful process of self discovery and one that will help you for the rest of your working life.

Skills are undeniably a vital ingredient for success in all job roles and for some the more specific or the more transferable the better. For some very specialist, technical and clinical jobs, having exactly the right skill set and proven ability to do the role could certainly be the determining factor. I'm sure you wouldn't want to be operated on by anything other than a top quality brain surgeon! However, *your true marketability* is your complete package of:

- Skills
- Attributes
- Attitude
- Strengths
- Achievements
- Knowledge
- Connections
- Interests
- Passions
- Values
- Personal Brand

Skills will always be important and the more transferable the better. However, as I have said, they do not provide the full picture. It is a fact that most skills can be learnt or developed and you can always plug skills gaps by going on courses or finding a mentor, as we will look at later on in the book. Conversely, when looking at attributes and attitude it is harder to change your personality, nature and outlook on life. The old adage that 'a leopard can never change its spots' is true to an extent. However, you **can change** but only by working really hard to develop and grow personally to have a positive impact on who you are and how you approach life. It is also a fact that 'you never get a second chance to create a first impression'. Therefore if what you see is what you get, then enthusiastic, positive people, radiating energy, become infectious, so why would you not want to be one too? These points all illustrate that your true marketability is so much more than your skills.

The Bigger Picture

Marketable means that you are sought after and in demand. Your true marketability is the value you offer an employer or the marketplace in terms of your complete package. You can now see by establishing your true marketability that **this is an infinitely more powerful proposition than just focusing on your skills**. Enthusiasm, determination, drive, energy, passion, willingness to learn and a positive 'can do' attitude can leapfrog you over the competition, even when they have more experience and 'better skills'. *Why?* Because such attributes and attitude can add real value to most jobs and organisations, whether this is for employed roles or to win work or contracts if you are self-employed.

So what do you have 'for sale' that you can offer to an employer or to your clients if you decide to set up your own business? If this sounds like a difficult question, don't worry, as we will go through a number of exercises to help you flesh out this key information. You can start to work on identifying your unique selling points or propositions (USPs). For USPs think *what makes you different or better* than your competition? Consider how difficult it would be for you to establish this without first having dug really deep, as we will do with some of the forthcoming exercises? I cannot stress this strongly enough, regardless of the level you are working at or aspiring to, the majority of people greatly undersell themselves. In today's fiercely competitive job market, by establishing and really accentuating your true marketability, you will stand out from the crowd. This also becomes of great importance when we look at your personal brand, at the end of this Chapter.

The following case study is an excellent example of getting to grips with your true marketability and being able to see the 'bigger picture', past your previous jobs, to get you ahead of the competition.

Julie's Story

Julie, married to a Brit, is a delightful French woman who was determined to settle down in the UK and carve out a career for herself and eventually start a family. Her career had previously been in a number of support roles but she had never found her true passion. Following her last role, which resulted in redundancy, she was frustrated and unsettled, so decided to travel round Europe with her new husband. What started as an adventure and escape from their dull working routine for a few months, turned into a few years of travelling and working their way around Europe. Eventually, they felt it was time to return, get back to reality, 'proper jobs' and get themselves on the property ladder.

When I asked Julie 'what was holding her back', she told me employers were not taking her seriously because they expected her to go off travelling again, so were not prepared to take the risk in recruiting her. In addition, she felt she was always falling short of the required skills highlighted on job descriptions, so either did not apply for some jobs or rarely got an interview. If she did get an interview, it became apparent to me that she was talking herself out of the job by her lack of belief in herself and what she had to offer. She also felt lacking in not having certain qualifications that were 'required' in some of the jobs for which she applied.

The turning point was getting Julie to open up and focus on some of the amazing experiences from her travels. Focusing on her achievements, the wide range of skills she had used, some of the weird and wonderful jobs she had done while travelling and above all else, her passion to work with disadvantaged people with learning difficulties and make a difference to their lives helped Julie see a new future. This was to become a new and very different Julie!

I worked intently with Julie and impressed on her that passion, desire, hunger, enthusiasm, positive attitude, willingness to learn and many similar attributes and attitudes could win the day against more experienced competition 'with the required piece of paper'. Julie was initially unconvinced and could not see past having the required qualifications. I shared with her similar examples of other clients I had worked with over the years who proved my point beyond all shadow of doubt. She realised she had classic limiting beliefs around her true marketability. What she had believed up to now was her perception rather than reality. This was her first breakthrough!

Julie then landed an interview for her 'dream job' at a local college, supporting young people with learning difficulties. However, she was still convinced she would not get the job and was only there to 'make up the numbers'. The fact that she had achieved an interview already proved my point that they considered her a strong candidate. Why would they bother otherwise?

Key point - You must have the core belief if you get invited to an interview that you have a fighting chance of getting the job. This is an important reframe, so you can show confidence, self belief and be positive in your ability to get the job.

So, first part of the job done but Julie now had to nail the interview. It is not my intention to cover interview skills in great detail in this book, as the focus is very different and there are plenty of other excellent books and resources readily available. However, I worked with Julie on answering key questions; especially the dreaded 'tell me about yourself', which is many people's nightmare question and maybe yours too?

Julie tended to ramble on about travelling Europe with her husband for the past few years. Instead, I got her to focus on what she had learnt from the experience, some of the skills she had developed along the way, how the experience had changed her thinking about life, how adaptable and flexible she had learnt to become and above all else, how she was now passionate about giving back and making a difference to the lives of less fortunate young people. What we did was to work really hard on her true marketability; i.e., the things that made her who she is and what she really had to offer in relation to the job. The result... Julie got the job! Not only did she get the job, she did so being the only person to make the shortlist who was not formally 'qualified'. This feedback was volunteered by the line manager who stated in no uncertain terms that, despite not having the desired (not required) qualification, Julie blew the interview panel away with her amazing passion and enthusiasm, but most importantly her willingness to learn and genuine desire to make a difference.

What a great result and amazing transformation. This case study encapsulates so much of what I have covered in the first two Chapters in terms of the power of your thinking and mindset.

Unlock Your True Potential!

"Your attitude, not your aptitude, will determine your altitude"

Zig Ziglar - Author and Motivational Speaker

I love this wonderful quote from the enigmatic Zig Ziglar, an inspirational personal development guru, who unfortunately passed away as I was writing the book. I believe his quote exemplifies what can be achieved if you really understand your true marketability because then you can sell yourself with maximum effectiveness, impact and confidence. You are learning some important lessons from these inspiring case studies so let's now build on this and take a look at some great ways to flesh out your true marketability and really unlock **your** potential.

How? Where Do I Start?

The starting point is to identify your natural talents and also hidden talents. This is often a revelation as you discover things about your skills, attributes and attitude that you may never have considered. The process of self discovery should also give your confidence a great boost! To help you achieve greater clarity of who you are and what you have to offer, the Proudest Achievements and Self Awareness Matrix are powerful exercises to help you unlock potential and passions you may not have considered.

✎ *Exercise - Your Proudest Achievements*

Do you ever think back to when you were 'invincible' or when you achieved something significant or remarkable in your life? In my case, it was when I was 23 and decided to up sticks and travel to Australia. The whole planning process, my amazing adventures, challenges and experiences undoubtedly helped to change my life and shape who I am today. Regardless of what stage you are at in your life, I would like you to reflect and identify some of your proudest achievements. This is a very powerful exercise if you apply yourself by being totally committed to the task, as you need to be with the entire Career Navigation Cycle process. So here we go:

Step 1

Clear your mind and consider a couple of your favourite achievements. These should be things that you are very proud of and make you feel good thinking about them. They should be personal to you so don't worry about whether other people think these are your 'best' achievements as it is important to choose what feels right for you.

Note – only one achievement should be work related and one (or more) totally non work related. *Why*? - Because it is usually the achievements outside the workplace, which reveal the skills, attributes, attitudes, knowledge, learning and so on that can help to uncover your hidden talents, unlock your potential and open up new thinking and opportunities!

Step 2

Write up each achievement as a short story in whatever way works best for you e.g. using your computer or on a sheet of paper using the following process:

- What you set out to do and WHY
- The challenge - what was in your way
- Step by step - what was your approach
- The result - what was the outcome of your efforts
- The meaning - how did it make you feel

Step 3

When you have completed each story, read through and list as many skills and attributes as possible that you feel you demonstrated in the process of your achievement. You will more than likely find this difficult (it is!) but persevere, as you will gain much benefit from the output.

Step 4

To gain another perspective and add to your list of skills and attributes, share your stories with people you know, trust and value their opinions and ask them to list skills, attributes, attitudes and even knowledge. You might just be surprised what they come up with!

Step 5

Now consider what you have learnt from this exercise. What is the output telling you? Also, how do you feel having fleshed out such useful and positive information about yourself? If you are like the vast majority of people who do this exercise, you will come to realise it is always much harder for us to see the good in ourselves. It is always easier to see others' good qualities. Also, we often overlook the obvious as we 'can't see the wood for the trees!'

✎ *Exercise - The Self Awareness Matrix*

Let's now continue building the picture with another great exercise that will really challenge your thinking and help to unlock your potential and passions. This exercise may look innocuous but it helped to transform my thinking and has done the same thing for many of my clients. *Why?* For a couple of simple but key reasons:

1. Just because you are good at something doesn't mean to say you enjoy it the most

2. You may have never considered your passions and interests could be potential income opportunities!

Note: You will find some useful video clips explaining this exercise and others from this Chapter on my Steve Preston YouTube channel:

http://www.youtube.com/channel/UCj0dyVi9gborbV0fLSZ7iow/videos?view=0

Attracts/Interests/ Inspires (Passions)	***Best at***
Experience package (skills, knowledge, attributes/attitude)	***Enjoy most***

Unlocking your Potential and Passions: the Self Awareness Matrix will help you uncover:

- What attracts, interests and inspires you
- What you most enjoy doing
- What you are best at

- Any additional knowledge, skills or attributes
- Recurring themes from your career and life thus far
- What you enjoy and want to continue doing
- What you enjoy and maybe don't want to continue doing
- A whole raft of possibilities to consider and review!

Step 1

You can set this matrix up on a Word document or similar on your computer or use a minimum A4 size sheet of paper, as you will need plenty of space to write in each quadrant.

Step 2

Completely open your mind and be prepared to stretch your thinking. You now have a blank canvas to create something new and exciting! **Think about all aspects of life not just work.**

Step 3

Start writing in the quadrant you relate to the most or you find easiest and use words or statements that reflect how you feel e.g. **Enjoy The Most** might be helping people

Step 4

The Experience Package quadrant is the only one that is 'absolute' i.e. this is related to skills and attributes from your career and life. You can transpose the skills and attributes you have fleshed out from the Proudest Achievements exercise plus any others that now spring to mind. Also, specific knowledge you have that is clearly part of who you are.

Step 5

Keep adding words and statements in each quadrant till you run out of steam. **If you feel a word or statement fits in more than one quadrant add it to each one it applies to.** This is very important as it is sending you a powerful message you should not ignore.

Step 6

Keep challenging yourself and drill down to another level e.g. if you had 'helping others', what is it about helping others you enjoy the most or are best at? This way you will get even more specific information you can then work with.

Step 7

Look for the common themes that appear in multiple quadrants, especially 3 or all 4. These are really important as you are getting powerful messages that you ignore at your peril!

Step 8

As with the Proudest Achievements exercise, ask trusted, valued friends and contacts to tell you '*what you are best at*'. Make the point that this is not just about work but anything they feel relevant about you as a person in life in general. Add their comments to your matrix. If you find this exercise too difficult to complete on your own, I suggest you work with a Coach or someone you can open up to who will ask you challenging questions around your story. It is important you keep adding to the matrix as you get new inspiration and 'light bulb moments'. This is a work in progress as you continue the book and work your way round the Cycle.

What have you got?

You should now have a whole raft of information about yourself which you can start to explore in more depth. What are the common themes in multiple quadrants? What are these telling you about yourself and possibilities for future jobs or work? Compare the output against your proudest achievements exercise and consider whether a picture is starting to emerge? Are there any surprises? If so what are they? Also, can you see themes emerging around skills and attributes which always appear when you achieve anything worthwhile or when you do work you love? This leads nicely into the next section.

The Importance Of Understanding Your Motivated Abilities

Your Motivated Abilities are your natural gifts or talents, things you gravitate to without even thinking e.g. favourite skills and attributes. Other ways of looking at your motivated abilities are: Your inner motivation, what makes you tick and depending on your outlook, some people also use terms such as, 'your natural DNA' and 'your unique calling'. These are the skills, attributes and recurring strengths that are always at the heart of any achievements in your life. By understanding these motivated abilities you can make sure they feature in your everyday work in the future. This way you can create a fulfilling life and maximise your true potential. I'm sure this sounds appealing, doesn't it?

✎ *Exercise - Motivated Abilities*

The good news is you can now start to uncover your motivated abilities using the output from the previous two exercises. Now to dig even deeper with this simple but effective exercise!

1. Look at your list of skills and attributes and consider which of these you can now see are the ones you naturally gravitate towards and feature when you are at your happiest. Also, those which, on reflection, you realise always feature when you have achieved anything worthwhile in your life.
2. Highlight these skills and attributes so you can start to focus your energy on them. Imagine how you can use them in a different environment, career or type of work.
3. Also now consider other skills and attributes you naturally use, which if they did not feature in a future job or career, would seem like you were missing a key part of you.

You now have some immensely powerful information about yourself that is a key part of your true marketability and which can help to shape your future!

📖 *Mo's Story: We all have a tendency to 'undersell' ourselves, but this is the greatest!*

I will now share with you a most extreme example of someone who was blissfully unaware of their true marketability. This is an inspiring story of a client who had some amazing hidden talents and motivated abilities and how by uncovering these, his thinking changed and then he changed his life. Please read carefully, as you, like Mo, could take the learning from this story to change your life. That would be an amazing feeling, wouldn't it?

A number of years ago I was running one of many workshops for unemployed professionals and executives. I had just introduced the concept of the 'Self Awareness Matrix' to the group. They all understood what needed to be done except one person who challenged me by saying, *'I cannot think of anything outside of work and I know there is no work to be had in my field in the UK as it is so specialist, so what else can I do to make this exercise work for me?'*

I was aware that Mo had come over to the UK from the US post 9/11, when he did not have the right papers. Mo did work in a very specialist field of fire protection and there was only one company in the UK who did this type of work and they had no jobs available at the time. He had not found work of any sort and was really struggling to keep focused and motivated. I questioned him on what else he was attracted to, what he did outside of work, what hobbies he had and so on. The answer that came back was always *'nothing'* or *'none'*. Undeterred and not to be beaten, I then asked him if he did any work in the community or voluntary work. What you are about to read will hopefully, like me and all of group that day, blow your mind!

Mo shared with the group that he *'was involved with the refurbishment of his local mosque'*. I asked him what sort of activities this involved. Although this was a number of years ago, it is still fresh in my mind and went something along these lines:

He had to:

- Organise for planning permission with the local authority
- Help with drawing up the refurbishment plans
- Find a suitable building company to carry out the work

- Muster up a large team of dozens of volunteers
- Create a budget for the refurbishment
- Manage and monitor the budget
- Keep track of the work being done, etc, etc!

Then a couple of fantastic throwaway comments:

"And we managed to do everything on time and within budget" to which the group pointed out this never happens in 'the real world'! Then another real showstopper: *"I forgot I also organised the relaunch party in the park opposite. I contacted the Mayor, local press and media and organised a massive firework display. The Mayor opened the ceremony and thousands of people turned up including the local BBC news team who interviewed me for London News. It was a great success!"*

Watching everyone's body language in the room was unbelievable as most people were sitting totally spellbound with their mouths wide open like goldfish. I asked Mo what his story was telling us. One of the group chipped in and asked if he had considered taking up project management? Remarkably there was still confusion on his face and he replied totally seriously '*I wouldn't know where to start*"! By this time the room was full of laughter from total disbelief at his response before one of the group piped up saying *"you have just given us the most amazing example of successful project management, so what are you talking about!"* Only then did he register what was happening and he had the most amazing light bulb moment.

Mo shared that he had secretly thought about setting up a business with his wife, an interior designer and *"What if I went out finding and managing projects and she did the feminine soft interior touches?"* To say this was a career defining moment was the understatement of the century! It also proved, yet again, that most people have little idea of their true talents and capabilities and can only think of themselves in relation to the jobs they have done in their careers. This is another key reason why people undersell themselves so dramatically - they really don't understand what they do have to offer. Yet here was the most extreme example of someone blessed with some fantastic skills, attributes and an undeniable natural talent or motivated ability for managing projects. This was reconfirmed when Mo recalled other, much smaller projects, outside the workplace he had successfully managed in the past!

What can you learn from Mo?

One minute he was incapable of considering doing anything other than the job he had trained for his entire career and next minute he was visualising a new career, the joy of setting up a business with his wife and making a success of it! Truly amazing and I felt privileged to have facilitated and witnessed such an immediate transformation.

I have come across many similar examples where people are totally oblivious to skills and talents and attributes they possess. Mo's story proves emphatically, once you take the blinkers off and come to terms with your true marketability and motivated abilities the only thing that can stop you achieving a similar success is guess what? Yes... you!

In terms of the Career Navigation Cycle, Mo in one fell swoop had:

- Let go and was looking forward (Step 1)
- Understood what was important to him in his career and life and WHY (Step 2)
- Uncovered many of his hidden talents, passions and his true marketability (Step 3)
- Started to think about exploring new opportunities (Step 4)

This just shows how powerful the insights gained from his amazing achievement were, in proving to him that he did have lots of great skills and attributes. Therefore, if Mo could deliver such a massive project on time and to budget then anything was possible. This was invaluable reassurance, which is something we all need to motivate us and spur us on. In a flash Mo had moved 3 steps round the Cycle!

I'm sure you too have also had achievements in your life that you have just brushed over and taken for granted, rather than looking more closely to see how remarkable they really were? By taking the learning from such examples, you will challenge and change your thinking about what you have to offer the world and what work you can now consider. With this in mind, get cracking to see what inspiration and exciting light bulb moments you uncover!

Personal Profiling

How About Personality Or Psychometric Profiling?

Now you have uncovered your many skills, attributes and motivated abilities, is there an argument for you to also do some personality or psychometric profiling? If so, what is it and how might it help you? There are a multitude of personality profiling tools available these days, which can measure your behaviours, temperament, communication style, strengths, how you work in a team, leadership style and ability and many variations on these themes. Some can even be done free online. However, these are usually cut down versions of the full paid for profiles and often you will need to pay for the main report or follow up coaching.

Career Coaches, like me, will need to be trained and accredited before they can give professional feedback on such tools. Some profiles are only available from qualified psychologists. While many reports are fairly self explanatory, most of the real 'nuggets' are hidden in the information that is not obvious, so while freebies are OK, they will provide only a part of the picture. There are also some career profiling tools, which are aimed at narrowing down potential options for future careers. My experience of these is that they can often confuse rather than clarify and you can sometimes end up with an A-Z list of career options, like something out of a Monty Python sketch! Remember there is no 'holy grail' or quick fix.

For the full reports, in terms of recommendations, there are many well respected tools e.g. Myers Briggs and DISC which all measure different aspects of your behaviour, strengths, motivation and preferences. It is easy to get lost in the range of options. Although I am accredited for DISC, which I like because it is very transparent and has always proven to be very accurate, there are many advocates of Myers Briggs plus a raft of other profiling tools. You can see an example DISC report on my company website: **http://www.smp-solutions.co.uk/Personal/CareerPersonalDevelopment/PersonalityProfilingDISC.aspx**

How do these tools measure up against some of the exercises in this book?

Unlike the exercises you have completed in this book, which you can do in your own time and at your own pace, being honest and from your heart, it is important to understand that personality and psychometric profiling requires you to answer multiple questions within an allotted time e.g. anything from 10 minutes to 45 minutes depending on the complexity and number of questions. The nature of these profiles means you need to answer with your immediate gut reaction. Although it is good to trust your gut instincts, as we have covered previously, when you are bombarded with a raft of similar questions with multiple choice possibilities for answers e.g. strongly agree, disagree, etc, you can feel pressured to come up with an answer just to move onto the next question, so you tend to answer from your head rather than your heart.

Your mindset will also play a big part, so the results can be very contextual, depending on what stage of the 'emotional roller coaster' you are at. I tend to use such profiling sparingly, mainly when the client has never had experience of such analysis, so that these will be new revelations. Also, where they may have done profiling a while ago, they may be keen to see any differences. Unlike some of my previous bosses, I would never use such profiles in isolation to determine the fate of a member of staff!

For top professionals and executives, understanding your emotional intelligence (EQ) and how best to use this can be a great benefit. Many organisations are coming to the realisation that having high EQ is of greater benefit as a leader than high IQ. You only have to look at Sir Richard Branson and Lord Alan Sugar as two wonderful examples. Emotional Intelligence is a big subject in its own right but one I would recommend you learn more about if you want to know how to get the best out of your 'emotional capacity' to influence and impact on others. Do some research on the web plus also check the resources section at the back of this book.

Health Warning...

Although most profiling tends to be a fairly good assessment of the person, because of some of the concerns mentioned, some people berate such tools, as they don't believe them to be an accurate reflection of themselves. The reality might be that it is an accurate snapshot of you **in that moment.** I have found when clients have done such profiling during restructuring or as part of the redundancy selection process, the results are often skewed. You might be tempted to answer how you believe you want to be perceived by your employer rather than what you believe yourself. This rather defeats the object and you are ultimately going to get found out. Also, I would caution against thinking that by doing some personality profiling you will shortcut the Career Navigation Cycle process. The output from any profiling is only a small part of who you are and what you have to offer, so a fraction of your true marketability. Remember follow and believe in the process. There are no shortcuts and more haste = less speed!

Brand 'YOU'

We have looked at many aspects of your true marketability, all of which are crucial in helping you understand more about yourself and what you have to offer to help you navigate your way to a brighter future. In the final piece of your true marketability jigsaw, we will explore the importance of your Personal Brand and how to make this work for you.

I have said consistently throughout this book, that the majority of people greatly undersell and under value themselves. By developing your personal brand, you have an opportunity to be much clearer about the authentic you and what you have to offer the world. Developing your personal brand therefore should be a key part of any self marketing strategy, regardless of whether you decide to look for a new job, become self employed or develop a portfolio career.

Personal Brand – Stand Out From The Crowd

Personal branding is about what makes you unique or 'remarkable'. It relates to how people see you, what you project to others and their perception of you. The key to building your brand is therefore to know yourself and aim to be the best possible you!

Your personal brand identity is about:

- Your image
- How you look
- Your behaviours
- How you communicate
- Your reputation
- How you make others feel
- The impact you make

We have already covered the fact it is so much easier to see things in other people than it is in ourselves. This makes it all the more important to get the right feedback on how people really do perceive you from a number of perspectives. Understanding, developing and managing your personal brand builds on the work you have already been doing in this Chapter. Your future career depends on your ability to effectively communicate you, your thoughts and ideas in a confident, clear and compelling way. Imagine the difference this will make for you at interviews, when networking or in client meetings? Much more confident, I'm sure.

The best way to market and position yourself is by developing your personal brand, as the better you are at getting your personal brand to work for you the less you need to sell yourself. Let's face it, selling ourselves is what most of us hate doing, isn't it? That said, having a branded message, which is authentic about who you are and what makes you distinctive, will be an important ingredient to your success. However, at this stage of the Cycle, you might not be ready to launch your branded message out to the universe, might you? This is more than likely another work in progress, isn't it? If so, why not play with such messages and test them out on family, friends and close contacts first to gauge their reaction. You can fine tune your message over time, as you will be in a much better position to have developed an authentic message you feel comfortable and confident with by the time you complete this book.

To define your personal brand identity you have to discover who you are and what differentiates you. You have already covered much of this work in previous exercises in this Chapter and Chapter two. Your personal brand identity is an amalgamation of your assets (skills, attributes, natural talents and life experiences), your values (the things that matter to you) as well as your passions and your image (what you project to others). Importantly, it is also how you look, behave, sound and how you make others feel. It's what you measure everything you do against, for example:

- How you meet and greet people
- The way you react or respond to others
- How you follow up
- How you listen
- Your empathy with others
- How you manage colleagues
- The questions you ask
- How you come across in presentations
- How you run meetings
- The way you dress
- How you engage others
- Your outlook on life
- Your overall persona

Your brand identity is what makes you stand out from the crowd, as an individual. With modern technology, your brand identity is also about your 'communication tools' e.g. your Smartphone, iPad, tablet or laptop. Are you an Apple, Blackberry or Android person and why? Also your networks, how you develop and manage these is of utmost and increasing importance. We will look at how you manage your online reputation through social media and blogs in Chapter 4. In summary, the definition I like best is *"your personal brand identity is what people say about you when you're not in the room"*. This says it all, don't you think?

Ask Others You Know, Trust & Value

Personal Brand Development, to bring you to life in a compelling way, is a relatively new concept in the UK. It has attained a much higher profile in the US to date, but things are now changing, as the global marketplace becomes ever more competitive. In order to really explore your personal brand, you also need to know yourself from the feedback from others. For some of the questions related to the exercises in this section, it will pay you to ask the same people you have asked previously for feedback, especially the Self Awareness Matrix and Proudest Achievement exercises. This way you can look for consistency from trusted and valued contacts.

If you are looking to progress your career you tend to be more aware of the fact that you need to do something positive about managing your image and reputation. If you are changing career completely, then the same is also true. *Why?* Because you could be known for having a career, in, let's say, the IT industry and are seen as a particular type of person. If you now decide to change to a completely different career or start your own business, this suddenly puts you in a very different light. You will almost certainly need to project yourself in a different way to create maximum impact. This is why so many people hold back from making such a change, as the thought of reinventing yourself and your brand can be quite scary, as we saw with Jane in Chapter one. However, you don't want to be like this do you? I thought not! Therefore, you will need to work through these exercises and gradually develop your new personal brand identity over time, as you find your new life path.

✎ *Exercise – Creating Your Personal Brand Using The 5 P's*

Defining your personal brand

As a starter to the main exercise, write down key words or statements which you believe reflect who you are and what you have to offer, that you believe are the authentic you.

Ask yourself does your personal brand have the right impact to aid your success, your new career choice (if you have one) or does it undersell you?

This is a big area and one where it really pays to work with a personal branding and impact coach. Debbie Smith, who works with executives and professionals, is a specialist in this field and also a key associate in my company team.

Personal Branding is a big subject, so for this book, we will focus on **Purpose, Passions, Personal Presence, Perception and Product.**

Defining your vision and purpose

To build your brand you must have a clear picture of who you are, where you're going and how you're going to get there. As you might have gathered this is not an easy task but stick with it, as you will reap the rewards.

You may not have a clear picture of your vision yet, but if you do, write it down somewhere you can see it. You can then constantly and regularly revisit it to motivate yourself to achieve the goal.

(i) Your Purpose

A great exercise to help you to establish this is to imagine yourself at your own funeral. I know this might sound morbid but you will see why this can be helpful when you've done it. Imagine you can hear what people are saying about you, what you've accomplished, how you touched their lives, your legacy, how you made a difference to them. Their comments suggest your purpose. What are they saying about you? Write down what you're hearing. This can be very powerful to help you move forward. You may have never thought this way about your purpose before.

(ii) Your Passions

Your passions are the activities that most energise you. In addition to being perceived as a high performer, your passions will also make you memorable. Using the work you have done from 'Your Proudest Achievements' and the Self Awareness Matrix exercise, list 10 things which will make your life and work ideal. Then list your top 5. Put them in priority order of most passionate as number 1. Describe *'what does that look like?'* Describe each one in as much detail as you can. This will help you to bring your passions to life.

(iii) Personal Presence

"Like it or not people will always be judged on their appearance as well as their abilities and in the current climate some bosses will be reassessing their workforce, so it's prudent to look the part as well as acting it".

Professor Khalid Aziz,
Business Journalist & Author

Managing your appearance to direct attention to where you want it, from potential employers, clients and people in your own circles is essential in determining the success of your brand. When your image is polished and refined, your personal presence conveys a grounded and trustworthy person... someone with whom people want to interact with and do business. When your image is out of balance, your personal presence is compromised and may send unintended signals to the very people you want to positively influence. How you dress and your general presence says much about your person and needs to be consistent with the type of work and people with whom you mix.

(iv) Perception

What are others' perceptions of you as a person? How you look, behave, work, your image, reputation, and so on? **What do people say about you when you are not in the room?** Find out and write this down so you can work on this constantly as you move your career forward, regardless of what you end up doing.

(v) Your Product

To sell and market yourself successfully it really helps to think of you as a product. You need to create a desirable 'package' for your product that will make you remarkable!

How you package yourself, your skills, attributes, knowledge and talents will ultimately determine the effectiveness of your 'campaign', whether in or out of work.

- What are your special skills and talents?
- What are you selling to potential employers or clients if you plan to set up your own business? If you know, write it down and focus on it. If not, you can return to this later, once you have completed Steps 4 and 5 of the Cycle.

- **What makes you remarkable, different or better** than other people you are competing against? If you know, write it down and focus on it. If not, again you can return to this later, once you have completed Steps 4 and 5 of the Cycle.
- Is your product (i.e. you) appropriately priced?
- Do you understand your true worth or are you underselling or overselling yourself?
- Do you need to make improvements (e.g. acquire more skills) to command the salary or package you are aspiring to?

So many questions and not enough answers?

You may not know the answers to some of these questions at this stage of the process. Don't worry as it will pay you to revisit this section regularly, once you start to see a new picture emerging, or when you have completed the book and the six steps of the Cycle. The more work you do around your personal brand and creating an authentic you the more people will talk about you in glowing, positive terms when you are out of the room or online, and the greater your chances of achieving success in life. To put this into perspective, the following case study is a brilliant example. It encapsulates many of the key points from this Chapter around establishing your true marketability (including your personal brand) and how to use the learning from this 'work in progress' to successfully relaunch you and do work you love.

🕮 *Jes's Story - Turning your true marketability into opportunities*

A successful General Manager, Jes reached a pinnacle in his career by helping his company achieve a prized nationally acclaimed customer service award. His 'reward' was to be treated very shoddily by his employer which resulted in him taking them to an Employment Tribunal. Jes was 'lost 'and in a bad place after a spate of bad luck following his redundancy. He decided to take positive action and sought refuge on one of our early Breakthrough Career Change & Transition Masterclasses.

The '*Proudest Achievement*' exercise was to become an amazing catalyst for him. Jes holds the record for having six full pages of flip chart paper plastered around the wall with his skills and attributes. This was truly amazing! His immediate reaction was *"Is that me?"* Of course it was. We merely facilitated the process and helped Jes get all the information out on paper. You could see the immediate change in his demeanour and the light bulb came on as he was wowed by the amazing revelations. Yes, he could change and his possibilities were endless!

What followed is interesting because Jes was fighting against the evidence which suggested he had a great skill set to become a Consultant and maybe set up his own consultancy business. At the time, he felt that was a bridge too far and he couldn't see it at all. This was a limiting belief. Self employment was probably too scary when he had so many other challenges in his life.

One of his key passions, which emerged from the Masterclass, was writing, with which he had never really done anything. Having come away from the day with renewed confidence, energy, motivation and focus, he very quickly secured some freelance work, writing reviews for luxury hotels around the world. This was a fantastic way of bringing together his travel background and his passion for writing. It also belied his thinking that he couldn't be self employed and what a tough first 'gig'! Within a few months he was headhunted as Sales and Marketing Director for a UK hotel chain, which he saw as a natural progression for him and a 'safer' option, being in an employed role.

Interestingly, it took that experience for Jes to finally come to the realisation that he wanted to be in control of his own destiny and should be running his own business. A couple of years after attending the Masterclass, that's exactly what he did. Jes set up a leisure marketing company and is now doing very nicely, enjoying life once more, following his passions, developing new skills and a strong personal brand and I'm sure he will never look back.

What does Jes's case study prove?

For some people, although all the evidence suggests self employment and setting up a business of your own, as in Jes's case, the timing may not be right for you. However, once the seed has been planted, this is bound to be your final destination. Park it for now but keep it in your sights as a medium or longer term goal while you explore other opportunities.

Following the steps of Career Navigation Cycle can have a profound impact. The process of self discovery can prove a massive boost to your self confidence and self esteem. This is especially so when you unlock your potential to establish your true marketability. You then realise that you have far more to offer the world than you think. This will empower you, enable you to promote yourself in the best possible light and will help you to start building your personal brand whether you wish to be employed or self employed.

How are you feeling about yourself now and what you have to offer the world? With your new found insight, like Jes, Julie and Sarah, you too can reinvent yourself.

Summary

- Your true marketability is your 'complete package', so much more than your skills
- Unlock your potential to uncover who you are and what you have to offer the world
- Establishing and understanding your true marketability is key to winning through redundancy and a successful career transition and can be a massive personal boost
- Avoid the 'scattergun' - resist the temptation to shortcut the Cycle process and fire out your CV before you have done the real hard graft and 'soul searching'
- More haste = less speed
- Skills are important but even more so are your attributes and "*Your attitude, not your aptitude, will determine your altitude*"
- Your motivated abilities are your natural talents. They will always appear as recurring themes of successes

and achievements. Get to know and love them and embrace them to lead a fulfilling life

- Don't be held back by your limiting beliefs about what you have to offer
- If the evidence is staring you in the face, don't ignore it but work with it to determine your short, medium and longer term goals
- Passion, desire, enthusiasm, positive mindset and all these great attributes can win the day against more experienced and 'skilled' competition
- Personality profiling is helpful and part of your marketability but not the answer to everything
- Work from the inside out - use your heart first then your head and be true to yourself
- Ask for honest opinions from others you know, trust and value to help answer key questions in order to establish your true marketability and personal brand
- Your personal brand is important - while you are still working never stop developing your brand, as it is what sells you

Congratulations, you have come to the half way stage of the Career Navigation Cycle! You now have lots of fantastic information about yourself to really challenge your thinking. You are now ready to move to Step 4 of the Career Navigation Cycle – **Exploring Opportunities**. Before you do this, let's look at what we have covered on the journey so far:

- Step 1 - you will have learnt how to 'let go' and move forward

- Step 2 - you will now have a much better understanding of what is important to you in your career and life and WHY this is important to you
- Step 3 - you have uncovered who you are and what you have to offer the world!

Before you move on to Chapter four, I suggest you might want to pause for breath and review all the good work you have done to date. **Reflection and review** is a key part of the career transition process. Often you will start to see things in a different light when looking a second time. However, it is your CHOICE, as it is important to work at your own pace and build momentum in the way that works best for you.

If you are finding the going tough at this point and you want some more inspiration to keep you on track, you might want to consider investing in my 4 CD or MP3 set audio book *'I Want A Career Change'* which you can access via this link:

http://www.stevepreston thecareercatalyst.com/index.php/i-want-a-career-change

Alternatively, if you want to work through things online at your own pace, my innovative *'I Want A Career Change'* online Career Change and Transition programme, will really help bring this book to life for you. As a thank you for buying this book, I am offering readers, a very special **discount of one third off (£100)**, which I know you will appreciate. Check it out via this link:

http://www.stevepreston thecareercatalyst.com/index.php/i-want-a-career-change/online-programme

You will need to show **WTR100** in the Coupon box on the shopping cart.

CHAPTER 4

Exploring Opportunities – Step 4

"You have to go into the dark to find the gold"

You have reached the half way stage of the Cycle. This is where you need to harness all the information and wonderful nuggets you have learnt about yourself from Steps 1 to 3 of the process, combined with focus on the 'outer self' career development part of the Cycle. It's important that you up your game, as you will be constantly challenging yourself to bring the pieces of the jigsaw together to help you ultimately decide what to do. This is likely to involve some difficult decisions, openly facing more of your fears and possibly breaking the pattern of conditioning which might have been ingrained from many years of work, parental thinking and influences from your friends and peers.

For many people this part of the process can become daunting because you've never had to dig this deep before. Although you have lots of powerful information to work with and may have come up with some great ideas, it is natural to experience self doubts around your ability to make change happen in the way that's right for you. If so, don't worry as this Chapter will guide you through what works and what doesn't. You will learn key techniques to help you explore and open up new opportunities, as it is unlikely you will want to be in the same position in six months' time, will you?

In this Chapter we will explore:

- How you can put your ideas into place
- How to find the right opportunities for you
- How to sell your 'new' self in the best way
- How to tap into the hidden job market
- The importance of social media
- Developing and optimizing your online and offline networks

- How to overcome your fears
- Some key mistakes to avoid
- Some key strategies to keep you focused and on track
- Turning talents and passions into profits!

Slotting Together The Pieces Of The Puzzle

Moving Through The Darkness And Towards The Light

You can now see that having established your true marketability and having a good handle on who you are and what you have to offer an employer, that you're in a much better position to start to think about pulling your CV together, *if* this is still relevant for you. Now is also the time to explore different types of jobs, careers and work you may have considered in the past but never had the courage to do anything about. In order to do this you need to be focused and set your priorities, as you can't do everything at once. By following the cycle you will feel excited, motivated, confident and eager to explore opportunities and reinvent yourself!

You may by now have a clear idea of what's next for you, maybe a number of options you'd like to explore before you decide or you might still be totally in the dark. This is not uncommon. How advanced you are with your new thinking is not so important at this point. *So, what should you be doing at this stage? What are some of your options?*

Unravelling the clues

Having come this far you must now start to challenge what the output from all the exercises so far is telling you. Consider carefully how you can use this knowledge to determine your next step. First and foremost, revisit, reflect and review the key exercises from Chapters one to three because you may see things in a different light second time round. As previously mentioned, reflection and review are key components of the career transition process. To help you further unravel the clues, gain focus and clarity to move from the Darkness to the Light, you now need to:

- Get out there
- Meet people
- Research
- Network
- Challenge your thinking
- Dip a toe in the water
- Be opportunistic

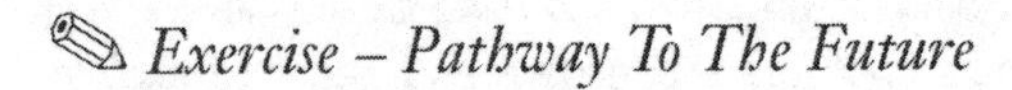

Exercise – Pathway To The Future

To help you move forward, let's look at some key questions you need to ask yourself:

	Question
1	(a) Do you still definitely want to be employed? (b) If so, do you know what type of job you would like to do yet?

2	Where might you apply your skills, attributes and values?
3	Have you thought about a particular company or organisation?
4	Does a particular type of environment or sector appeal?
5	(a) Are you still looking to progress your career? (b) If not what would 'downscaling' mean for you?
6	(a) Have you had enough of working for other people? (b) If so, do you like the thought of being your own boss and working for yourself?
7	If you start up your own business what can you do?
8	(a) Have you thought about changing the 'JOB' mindset altogether and considered a portfolio career? (b) How does changing your working lifestyle by deriving income from tapping into your talents, interests and passions appeal to you?

As you can see, these are some very big questions which you may well find quite daunting. However, I will guide you through the process, just as a set of traffic lights will take you safely across a major junction: to help you get the best out of this step of the Cycle, so you can move confidently onto step 5 and decide what to do.

But *What* To Do? *What* Approaches Are There?

At this stage of the cycle there are three broad areas for you to consider.

(i) To ensure you ***STOP*** making the most common mistakes

(ii) To consider some basic development options to get ***READY*** for a brighter future

(iii) To reflect on some simple points you can ***GO*** for now

(i) What To Avoid. STOP!

Impatience – Break things down into manageable chunks

It is only natural you will want to see results from your efforts so far. However, unless you have already come to some definite conclusions about what you want to do, until you have completed the next two steps of the Cycle it is unlikely you will see real progress. You have not yet started on the 'outer self' career development work to get to you to this point. A good strategy is to break tasks or activities down into bite size chunks so you can achieve 'small wins'. This is important to build momentum, keep you motivated and stay on track.

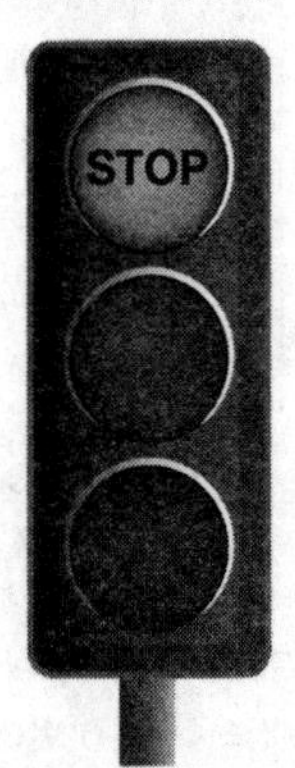

Sometimes you just need to 'be' rather than 'do'.

I find at this stage of the process, many people feel they need to be doing something all the time because they are used to the cut and thrust of everyday working life. However, it is often when you aren't looking for anything in particular that you will suddenly experience and appreciate what is staring you in the face, rather than frantically building up and completing your 'to do' list. Less is often more and by slowing down your mind, your intuitive feelings and inner voice will often give you the insight you need.

'Being an extra in your own movie'

Another key mistake you might make at this stage of the process is to compromise and settle for second best. What do I mean by this? Essentially, if you are looking at a total career change or even a fairly similar job but in a different sector or environment, you can often make the mistake of underselling yourself and taking a lower level job on the basis of being new to the sector or the type of work. If you are lacking in confidence or self belief, this is easy to do and you will be playing into the hands of an exploitative employer. However, the work you've done around your true marketability should clearly highlight that you have much to offer, so never undersell yourself. Believe in your abilities, including being able to successfully reinvent yourself, so you can navigate your way to a brighter future.

Out of the frying pan into the fire!

It is all too easy to consider that doing the same type of job you did prior to your redundancy is your only option. Will you be headhunted for a similar opportunity to the job you did before, feel flattered and more inclined to jump at the first opportunity that comes along? However, you may never get a better opportunity to reinvent yourself. Having come this far round the cycle, unless you really challenge yourself further to explore what might be possible, you could easily be jumping out of the frying pan into the fire and you don't want to get burnt, do you?

Not setting your sights high enough

In setting your target or goal take heed of the following inspirational quote from Michelangelo, painter, sculptor, architect and poet (1475 – 1564): *"The greater danger for most of us is not that our aim is too high and we miss it, but that it is too low and we reach it."*. You may think looking for a similar job is the easy option as it saves further soul searching and really stepping out of your comfort zone. However, the reality is **you never achieve anything worthwhile in your life without stepping out of your comfort zone.** Therefore, why not grasp the opportunity while you can and think about doing something completely different?

Health Warning...

Just because you are good at something doesn't mean you enjoy it! Along with a 'scattergun approach', thinking that you must continue to do work you are good at even if you don't really enjoy it, ranks as one of the most common mistakes that people make following redundancy. This is something I learnt very early on my journey and it's a really important point to help you make a successful career transition and end up doing work you love.

Having completed the exercises in Chapter three, you will have uncovered a number of things you are best at and you enjoy doing the most. Equally, you might uncover things you are best at but don't really enjoy. If so, now is the time to challenge yourself to consider whether you wish to continue with such work as your main job or at all, because you do have CHOICE!

Not being true to yourself

It is often at this stage of the Cycle and the career transition process that you have a dawn of realisation that you were in the wrong job before. If *1 in 2 people is 'in the wrong job' and 2 out of 3 are 'unfulfilled',* have you thought about whether you were a square peg in a round hole previously? If you now feel you were, you don't want this to happen again, do you? I have met so many people who just stuck at their jobs because it was easier to stay in their comfort zone with the knowledge that they could pay their bills each month. This might work for a while but at some point you will reach a peak of frustration and 'the volcano will erupt'!

Wouldn't it be great if you started to reframe and change your attitude so that you see things in a very different light? I remember vividly a woman in one of my workshops, a number of years ago, suddenly blurted out *"You know what Steve, I now realise I've just wasted the last 20 years of my life".* When I challenged her as to what she meant by such a controversial statement, she said she now realised she had been untrue to herself and she really hated the job and work she had been doing and was definitely a square peg in a round hole. She was another example of someone stuck in 'the velvet rut', but what an awakening! All is not lost - remember, *"You cannot recreate the past but you can create an exciting new future."*

I meet many people, especially from the IT and Finance sectors, who openly admit they only did the job because it paid well. This might serve your purpose for a while but once your values change and you realise there is more to life than money, you face a source of constant and increasing frustration. Be authentic, true to your values and you will discover fulfilment.

Thinking you must apply for a JOB

Working as a Career Coach, I now know there are very definitely many alternatives and you always have CHOICE. The reality is that, following redundancy, the majority of people are conditioned to think and believe that they must have another job, because this is what they have had their entire career. Your parents, family and circle of friends will no doubt all be giving you advice at this stage mostly with the expectation that you will find another similar job. However, as in my situation and with many of my clients, *'if you have been there, done that and got the Tee shirt'*, maybe it's time to consign the old one to the bin and look for a new one? Do yourself a favour and stop applying for the same old jobs and instead **consider whether you actually want another 'traditional' job at all?**

Health Warning...

Don't let recruiters, 'head hunters' or other people control your future. Take control yourself and learn to become 'the architect of your own future'!

Many people fall into the trap of believing recruitment or executive search consultants will be their saviour, post redundancy, so place great or even total reliance on such people. I once had a client in a job search workshop, whose proud boast was that he was signed up with nineteen different recruitment agencies. He was most upset when the general consensus of the group was that he was wasting his time! Depending on what jobs you are aspiring to, build relationships with industry specific recruiters and executive search consultants. The key is to make sure they understand your true marketability and don't try to fit you into a box you have outgrown or no longer wish to be in. You must understand that their motivation is different from yours, because they work on high levels of commission from the company. This means that if you are a hot prospect they will be 'all over you like the proverbial rash' and talk to you as if they are your best friend. Unfortunately, if they find more suitable candidates, they will drop you like a stone and suddenly become harder to find than the 'Scarlet Pimpernel'. Recruitment consultants are part of the job search mix but like everything, there are good and bad. Learn to manage them rather than the other way round. I have developed a brilliant relationship with an executive search consultant who shares my values and business ethos. He always goes the extra mile and is happy to share his knowledge and experience to benefit his potential candidates, which is rarely the case. He has also taken the trouble to understand how I can support some of his candidates who are 'lost', following redundancy, restructuring or just need to rethink their careers. Therefore, if you do find a really good recruitment or executive search consultant they can be a key player in *'finding your gold'*. However, always remember **only you** can take full responsibility for your successful career change or transition.

(ii) What To Consider: ***GET READY***

There are a number of development opportunities worth pursuing that would not only help improve your personal skills but also enhance your employability. There are great benefits to be had from volunteering, gaining work experience, undertaking shadowing or work trials. All carry high success rates, but even if you subsequently do not get recruited by an employer, the very nature of getting

back into the workplace, utilising your skills, learning new skills, proving your work ethic, having a sense of purpose and feeling valued is often a massive boost to your confidence and self esteem. By taking advantage of these opportunities you give yourself an excellent platform to build from, something live on your CV (you don't have to say this was unpaid work, but you can show it as a short project) from which it becomes much easier to secure a job or determine what you want to do next.

The Power of Volunteering or Work Experience

As part of your career transition journey and to help explore opportunities, volunteering or 'work experience' can be excellent ways to dip a toe in the water to see if you enjoy a particular type of job. These opportunities may include working within a particular company or a totally different work environment e.g. an outdoor job instead of an office job, or a sales job instead of a back office support role. If you think that by volunteering you are just being exploited and you find yourself only focusing on the fact that you are working for nothing, reframe your thinking. I have worked with many clients for whom this approach has completely changed their perception and been the catalyst for achieving their successful career transition. So, what have you got to lose?

Victoria Pendleton, the legendary British female cyclist, retired from competitive cycling in 2012, after a glittering career, including winning many Olympic and World Championship Gold medals. When asked what she will do next her response was *"I have only been focused on my final Olympic goal. Now this is over, I will start to think about what I can do next and will look at doing some work experience to find out what I like"*. Shortly after this she became a candidate for the BBC's popular TV programme 'Strictly Come Dancing' and swapped her gold medal for gold sequins. A bold move and a risk, but one wonders what opportunities this 'experience' might present for her in the future.

The following case study is a brilliant example of someone who really has 'become the architect of their own future', the philosophy of this book. Jacqui's story illustrates how finding 'work experience opportunities', coupled with following the complete six step Career Navigation Cycle process can transform your life.

Jacqui's Story

When I first started working with Jacqui on her outplacement programme, by her own admission, she was *'lost in the fog'*. She had been a very successful IT Director in a global corporation but was clearly not passionate about IT and had no desire to return to the industry, or even the corporate arena. It was definitely time for a complete career and lifestyle change. Having started life in the Police force, her career had evolved by accident rather than design. She had known instinctively when the time was right to break out into the commercial world. Now, following her redundancy, she was keen to explore new opportunities in tune with her values, passions and interests, as she had gained a huge amount from Steps 1-3 of the Cycle.

When it came to exploring specific opportunities, like many people, she drew a blank. However, in reviewing some of her passions and interests, there were recurring themes around her interest in gardening, nurturing plants and flowers and maybe even setting up her own garden nursery. Jacqui admitted that she was prone to procrastination and knew she had to keep building momentum, so explored the possibility of getting work experience in a garden centre. She quickly found a contact, a manager of a local garden centre, who was keen to help and in no time she was 'in amongst it' and loving it!

The outcome: realisation that running a garden centre is a big commitment and maybe was better as a longer term objective. Moreover, if she became the owner, she would employ a manager to run the garden centre for her. Due to a back injury Jacqui struggled with some of the heavy work. However, she realised that there were lots of other lighter jobs and ways to earn money from her love of plants and gardening.

When I last saw Jacqui she had decided what to do and had taken positive action to set up a small hanging basket business, with a view to building other income streams in tandem. She had also signed up to a year long horticultural course to gain a formal qualification, whilst also getting hands on experience in another garden centre environment. Her work experience had proved to be invaluable. She was really happy and was now well and truly on the way to making a successful career change and doing work she loved.

Work Shadowing

Work shadowing is another useful option that allows you to find out what it is like to work in a different environment. It is therefore another excellent way to 'dip a toe' in the water to see whether the job, a particular company or an alternative environment is right for you.

A good example is another strategic IT director from the corporate world, who was struggling to find new opportunities with similar organisations following his redundancy. I encouraged him to change his mindset and rethink his job search strategy. He decided to change tactic and explore whether working for a small company, where he would have much greater autonomy, would work for him. He researched companies within easy commuting distance, establishing the names of the managing director and chief executive. Next he made targeted, speculative approaches explaining his situation and his objective, in a very positive way. Within a very short space of time he had opened up opportunities with a couple of small businesses who agreed to him doing some work shadowing. The result: one of the companies recognised his true marketability and offered him an excellent role which he was delighted to accept. After a number of fruitless months job searching, his work shadowing strategy was clearly a great success. He quickly established that he would enjoy working in a smaller business and would thrive in an environment where he could really make a difference. He could also be true to his values, in contrast to working in a large corporate, who perceived him as being past his sell by date!

Work Trials

If you are signed on at your local job centre, Work Trials is an excellent scheme run by Job Centre Plus (JCP) that provides you with the opportunity to undertake work experience without losing your benefits. Although the rules and regulations often change, my experience is that it is your responsibility to source an opportunity with a local employer. JCP then acts as your sponsoring organisation to formalise the required paperwork. Although these are on an unpaid basis you may be able to receive general travel and lunch expenses. As with many schemes run by JCP, this is often on a 'need to know basis' so it is unlikely they will volunteer this information. Ask your JCP Adviser for details, if you are interested, as what have you got to lose? You might even gain really useful experience or a job, like my previous example!

(iii) What To Embrace Now. ***GO!***

What other approach can you adopt now?

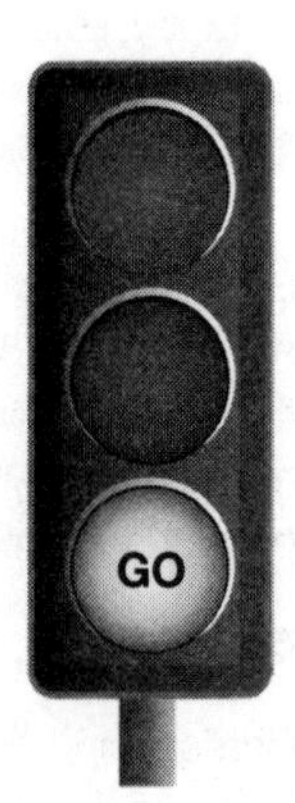

Although it is alien to most people to even think it, one of the first considerations is **do you actually want another job i.e. an employed role**? Now is the time to challenge yourself and step out of your comfort zone. You don't have to do what you did before, even if you have done it for years and you are good at it. Remember, you do have CHOICE!

Listen to your inner voice – follow your gut!

In Chapter one I talked about your inner voice. As a result of my experiences job searching, with recruiters, my 'scattergun approach' and negative interview experiences, my inner voice was niggling away at me asking the same questions over and over:

- What are you doing?
- Why are you putting yourself through this awful job search process?
- Why are you going to these interviews?
- Do you really want the job anyway?

- Do you really want to travel so far to work?
- Do you want to spend your life commuting daily on horrendous motorways?
- Is there another option?
- Do you want to work for another boss?
- Do you really want another job at all?
- Why don't you become your own boss?
- What do you really want out of life?

So many questions and so few answers! Do **you** recognise any of these thoughts? If so, I empathise. Don't make the same mistakes I did by letting your head rule your heart. Instead, embrace what your instincts, values and passions are telling you.

Be bold

Challenging yourself on the questions coming from your inner voice to follow your gut instincts, can help you open up a whole new way of thinking. You can rule out work you may no longer be interested in doing, whilst gaining more clarity about what you do enjoy and what to focus on.

In my last employed role, I was Rewards & Benefits Manager in my Company. Everyone said: *"You're really good at this stuff Steve, great at designing pay schemes, developing benefits initiatives, incentive schemes and all this associated activity."* Did I enjoy it? I enjoyed the end result, I enjoyed seeing the results of my efforts and the impact it had on the company and benefits to all the staff. Being true to myself and looking from a different perspective, there was a lot of boring, mundane work including number crunching and analysis which is just not me. I quickly came to the conclusion that I didn't want to continue with the Reward and Benefits work. It was time to change and move on. This was another career defining moment for me and I only did such work as a part of my portfolio career when I started my business, which I will cover in Chapter five. If you also feel this way about the work you have done previously then be bold and move on and reap the benefits.

Focus on what you want – intent

Thinking back to The Law of Attraction, one of the most important aspects of this is focusing on what you **do** want rather than what you **don't** want. Although it is helpful to rule things out and it is often easier to do so at this stage, by focusing heavily on what you don't want you will probably manifest just this. It is so important to remember *you are what you think and feel.* Therefore, focus your energy wholeheartedly on achieving what you do want. Think about your intent and focus on this and I'm sure you will find this much more energising. Clear out your negative thinking and review some of the work you have done already around your success criteria; the Values, Needs, Skills, Attributes and Motivated Abilities you fleshed out which are likely to provide clues here.

If you are still unclear on what it is you do want, and many people do get stuck on this, you need to set your intent to *'I want to know what I want'.* Although this may seem somewhat strange, by setting and focusing on this desire, you will begin attracting information, you will begin attracting people and opportunity; you will begin attracting many things to select from. Over time, from the steady stream of ideas that will flow your way, you will get a better idea of what you specifically desire. There are many books and resources which explain this amazing law of the universe. *'The Secret' (Rhonda Byrne)* is without doubt the most well known. It has become a cult book and film, having achieved worldwide success and recognition, especially after Oprah Winfrey dedicated a complete TV show to it.

'The Missing Secret' is also an excellent audio programme (CD/MP3 etc.) from Dr Joe Vitale, which focuses on the Law of Attraction in a big way. Joe Vitale was also featured in the film of *'The Secret'* but he felt, as good as the book and film were, there was a missing link. This is around the aspect of *'clearing'*, which I have alluded to in terms of clearing out your negative thinking. He also covers in more depth the importance of taking positive action, which we will explore in Chapter six.

I have only come to understand and see firsthand the power of The Law of Attraction, since I immersed myself in Personal Development. I could also see the strong link and benefits to Career Development, especially at key times of change in life, such as following redundancy. As with the Cycle, it is important to believe in the process. Your positive thoughts and emotions will generate positive energy to let the universe take care of the rest!

Keep an open mind

While you are exploring opportunities, you may make definite decisions, as with some of the examples, but you will be more likely to be ruling things in or out as you research. Therefore, it is important to keep an open mind. Ideas will often come to you in the most unlikely moments and can be triggered by conversations with people, something you see or read and I certainly would like to think from this book.

Core belief

As I mentioned in Chapter two, ***"If your WHY is strong enough the WHAT and HOW will follow"***. To explain this statement, if your sense of purpose and why you want to change career, be your own boss, progress your career or downscale your career is strong enough, the specific what you do next and how you will achieve it will follow. This is all part of your career transition journey and the Cycle process, so **you must be patient and go with the flow.** Don't be tempted to take short cuts. Keep following the process to be successful!

Become a detective

By becoming a detective I do not mean you should consider a career with the Criminal Investigations Department. Become adept at researching and sourcing key information to help you evaluate potential jobs, work or careers plus learning where to find useful information. Explore a variety of websites, reference books, professional associations, online forums and through the development of new contacts who can steer you in the right direction.

Visualise your goal

If you already have your end goal in mind e.g. setting up your own business but are unsure in what area, as with your 'vision of success exercise', you can cut out pictures to make a collage or draw something that represents your vision. Writing down key statements will give you constant daily focus. Alternatively, you may find online vision boards, such as Pinterest, more powerful. These are also a great way of piecing together ideas to help shape your future. For those of you who are very visual, visualising your goals is an effective strategy to help open up your thinking and explore new opportunities.

Visualisation is a fantastic skill which can help you achieve many positive outcomes for the rest of your life. Like learning any new skill, visualising takes practice and discipline but you will reap the rewards if you persevere.

Dr Lee Pulos is a renowned Guru in the art of visualisation. His audio book, '*The Power of Visualisation – Seeing is Achieving*' is recognised to be one of the best reference materials on this subject.

Developing your CV, bios and profiles

You now have enough information to start building a powerful CV by using much of the information you have gleaned from your true marketability coupled with understanding your values and needs. It is not the purpose of this book to focus in great detail on how to write a good CV as there are dozens of such books available, together with a plethora of online information. However, it is important at this stage to ensure you really flesh out the key information from the exercises in Chapters two and three, which will help you stand out from the crowd.

The key is **you must bring yourself to life** on all your paper and electronic marketing materials e.g. CV, bios and online profiles to best promote and enhance your personality, character traits, attitude, work ethic, key skills and achievements. In two pages of quality information, make sure your true marketability and personal brand shine through. Your key objective from creating a compelling CV is to give a potential employer a great reason to invite you to an interview and it will also put you in good stead for any volunteering, work experience or work shadowing opportunities. Although it may seem obvious, in a nutshell, your CV is to get you on the interview *'yes'* pile, yet many people forget this!

Let's look at how you achieve this objective, as what I am about to share with you is unlikely to be written this way in any other CV reference material but it works!

- The first key point is your CV is not written for you but for a potential employer so it must excite them

- Consider your CV must pass two tests to be in with a chance: the '10 second' and the '*So What*?' tests
- The first half page must compel the reader within 10 seconds to want to review the remainder of your CV
- The '*So What*?' test challenges the inclusion of typical bland and often unsubstantiated statements you may have made about your skills or attributes
- Most people's CV's have these, so your task is to restructure and rephrase such statements, like the example below
- Use positive language that focuses on your work achievements, contribution, skills and outcomes
- You are providing evidence of your competency, rather than what you have done

An example: skills statements should be one sentence and clearly contextualised, e.g. "*Excellent report writing skills producing meaningful executive summaries for Boards to make informed strategic decisions."* Isn't it clear that this is very different to just saying '*excellent report writing skills'* which most people would do, but doesn't pass the 'so what test'? With such a specific statement, I'm sure you would rather ask this candidate to an interview, wouldn't you?

Likewise, it pays to have monetary amounts, percentages, timescales and any other tangible measures to highlight achievements, especially in relation to improvements or cost savings. By taking this approach, you will also have some excellent ammunition for interviews!

Dino's Story

Although Dino worked at a high level in Sales & Marketing, he was the classic example of somebody who could sell 'ice to the Eskimos' but couldn't sell himself. Before we started working together, Dino had signed up to a large career management consultancy and invested an unnecessarily large amount of money. Unfortunately, despite his investment, after many months he was getting nowhere with his job search. *Why?* Simply because he hadn't done any of the 'inner self' work in Steps 1-3 of the Cycle, so he was at sea. Criminal really but that's another story. Consequently, Dino was blissfully unaware of what he had to offer, his very definite Values and Needs or his strong Personal Brand. As a result, his CV wasn't focused, targeted nor selling him in anything like the best light. He was pitching for the wrong jobs with no real strategy, based on his desire to land a new job quickly, instead of exploring in more depth what the job entailed and whether these jobs were in tune with his Values and Needs. Another classic example of a scattergun approach!

The solution: we had to go back to square one and once he had completed Steps 1-3 of the Cycle, Dino gained real focus and clarity. I then worked with him on his CV, which had been way too upmarket and 'flowery', to become a true representation of him (very genial and down to earth) and really brought him to life. Now his CV was very targeted and focused, he started receiving interest from companies and was able to sell himself confidently at interviews. The end result: Dino was in the enviable position of having two job offers. He based his decision on his

Values & Needs, landed a fantastic job that he loves, which has proved mutually beneficial for him and his company and is also an excellent launch pad to progress his career.

Be Opportunistic - Speculative Applications

Something I constantly encourage my clients to be aware of is the importance of both spotting and creating opportunities. For instance, you may see a job advertised which you feel is not right for you, but you like the sound of the employer and maybe the environment. In such situations try the following approach:

- Contact the recruiting manager if they have one and not the HR department, as this can often be a 'black hole'
- Always establish the name of the recruiting line manager and target them personally either by telephone or email, as 'to whom it may concern', never works!
- Explain you have seen the vacancy advertised, you like the sound of the company but are interested in a different or maybe higher level role with more responsibilities
- Sound positive and enthusiastic and genuinely interested, as your tone of voice will be a giveaway!

Our daughter landed a brilliant management job by taking exactly this approach, as the advertised vacancy was a level below what she was seeking. She liked the sound of the company and they her and once they had secured suitable funding, they offered her the job opportunity she really wanted. So again this was a mutually beneficial win situation.

The same speculative approach can be taken if there are specific companies you wish to target who are not currently advertising vacancies. What is the worst that can happen? Being told there are no vacancies for your level? Instead, they may take your details and ask you to email your CV to keep on file. However, I have worked with many people who have turned such opportunities into job roles. The company were considering a similar role and the application helped to crystallise the need. As with many things in life, you can often be in the right place at the right time but to a large extent you create your own luck.

Turning around unsuccessful job interviews

Although it is understandable that you will be disappointed when you receive a negative response to a job interview, I have often seen how you can turn this negative into a positive. A short, polite and professional email to the key decision maker stating how much you enjoyed the interview, maybe the environment, what you heard about the company and their plans and how you would be interested in similar opportunities, can often pay dividends. Be bold - why would you not want to do this?

The most fantastic example I can recall was a woman who did exactly as I've highlighted. Much to her surprise, she received a phone call out of the blue a few months later from the company concerned. It transpired that the successful applicant had decided to relocate abroad and having been impressed by the enthusiasm and initiative she showed, they immediately contacted her to see if she was still available and interested in the job. Although she was exploring other opportunities, nothing concrete had emerged at this stage. She agreed to meet them again on the basis that if they still liked each other, the job was hers. Everything went to plan. Only the outcome was even better. The company had won a new contract in

Singapore and they asked her to head it up for them. As she was single and mobile, this was a dream come true! Therefore the key lessons here are:

- Be true to your values
- Apply for the right jobs
- Be opportunistic
- Be bold
- Be positive with your initial approach and any follow up

As you have done much of the hard work already by revisiting your values and needs you will now see much more clearly what jobs, companies or opportunities are right for you.

How To Avoid 'Walking In Treacle'

In this section we will be examining some of the areas that hold us back, where we get stuck and prevented from progressing and moving forward. Often when some progress is made it can feel like going 'two steps forward and one step back' and this can give rise to a growing sense of frustration, disillusionment and disappointment, often likened to 'walking in treacle'. But I will now offer you some ways to overcome this debilitating condition.

Face Your FEARS

In Chapter one, we looked at facing your fears. At this stage when you're exploring opportunities, do you find this is where you are now openly facing your fears as well? This is often the point where reality kicks in for many people, so keep reading, following the Cycle and enjoy your journey. Now is a good time to revisit the two acronyms for "fear" in Chapter one, which have really helped to change many people's perception about what "fear" really is. Sportsmen and performers will always want to get pumped up and get their adrenalin going before a big event. This is a key time of change for you, a key stage of the Career Navigation Cycle and transition process, so exploring opportunities and making your breakthrough is a big event for you, too, so your emotions will be high. Ask yourself the question:

Is your 'fear' related to feeling '*excitement* and *anticipation'*, in which case this is positive? Or is your 'fear' based on your beliefs you *'can't change'* or you are still '*fearful*' for other negative reasons?

The solution: you need to **give yourself permission** to express your fears, so you can face them. This way you can learn to reframe your fears and banish them, as we covered previously. For many people, giving themselves permission to express and work on their fears using the two acronyms from the exercise, is all that you need to change your perceptions. Try it and see how you get on. By the time you complete the book and the six steps of the Cycle you will be ready to move from 'fearful to fearless'. Don't worry if you aren't there yet, as you are still a work in progress and you will get there, won't you?

Pauline's Story

Pauline is one of our top executive clients. She was very daunted by the thought she would be leaving her past employed career behind. Like Jane, who is featured in Chapter one, she had major concerns about whether she could be successful in her own right, running her own consultancy. How on earth would she make it work? These questions come up time and time again for so many people:

- *"Why would anyone want to pay me to do that?"*
- *"There are so many other people out there, why would they want to pay me?"*

My answer is always the same: *"People were very happy to pay you for many years in your career previously so why would they not want to pay you now?"*

You've proved that you're an expert in your field, so you can do the same in your own business. Again, it's a shift of mindset. Once you realise and understand this, it's absolutely no different. In Pauline's case, she was considering undertaking a PhD in Performance Management and harboured a fear of *"How is this going to work, will I be accepted etc"*. As always this has proved to be an unfounded fear. Pauline is now thriving, with some great projects and clients and is enjoying her independence.

Use Your Time Wisely - Spend Your Day Productively

One size does not fit all. Therefore there is no absolute right way to spend your day while in career transition. However, as you can now see there are many options to help you explore opportunities. Whatever you do, try to avoid 'Knee Jerk' reactions to situations just because you think you should.

I've met many people over the years who were very disciplined. They got up at the same time as when they were employed and then spent an "eight hour working day keeping busy" doing as many activities as possible. However, this is often not the right approach. Spending hours every day on the Internet job searching is definitely not the most productive use of your time. It can be hugely demoralising, isolating and incredibly time consuming. But why do people do this? Mostly because it appears to be the easiest option, seems the right thing to do and it gives them a feeling of being productive.

The reality is that you are:

- Putting yourself in amongst all the competition
- Not giving yourself an opportunity to explore new avenues or really test the water for what might be possible in a new career

One of the biggest negatives for many people is facing the risk of multiple rejections and the equally frustrating 'black hole syndrome', where your applications disappear never having seen the light of day. What can be even worse is not getting responses at all. Being left hanging, not knowing, can be even more frustrating than getting a rejection.

All this frustration and angst can really knock the stuffing out of you, in turn knocking your confidence and motivation, just when you need it the most. Therefore, you need to reframe your thinking because, although your job applications are of utmost importance to you, employers' priorities will be completely different and as annoying as this is, you have to respect this. Importantly, the issue here isn't about procrastination and intentionally creating delay, it is about spending your time wisely and focusing on the *right* things. Whilst I admit and empathise that being out of work is unlikely to give you the same self motivation as being in work, you do need to feel that you are being productive and achieving something.

To focus your mind, consider - *what is the consequence and value of what I am doing right now?* This is a great way to decide whether you are spending your time wisely and productively on activities that are beneficial and will move you towards your end goal. If not, you have to question the validity of what you are doing and move onto something that will be more productive. Consider, when are you at your best? Organising your day around when you are most energised and focused makes a lot of sense. This way you will know when is best to get stuck into key activities, e.g. researching, job search, rewriting your CV, developing your online profile and networks. Likewise you will know when to take some downtime and just 'be'.

Energy Boosters And Drainers

In this difficult transition phase, especially when you are exploring opportunities, it is really helpful to know what gives you a much needed energy boost. Equally, consider what you should avoid, what has a negative impact on you and will drain your energy.

Let's look back to some of the pointers in Chapter 1, to help boost your energy:

- Surround yourself with positive people
- Consult personal development books, audio material (CDs, MP3s) and films and downloads
- Attend motivational seminars and webinars

These activities can also be a great source of motivation and inspiration. Audio material is excellent for playing in the car especially when you are stuck in traffic, on journeys to family, friends or an interview. Brian Tracy makes reference to this and talks about using your car as *'a university on wheels'*. I have a client who now only listens to personal development CDs whenever he is in his car. The impact on him has been remarkable, as he now feeds off the positive energy. He has turned his business and life around. Learning from personal development books, audio material and films means you grow personally, not academically, which will put you in much greater shape to tackle the challenges ahead for the rest of your life. I'm sure you will agree, this can only be of positive benefit to you?

For many people, going for walks, running or doing some form of exercise provides the necessary energy boost, but again everyone is different, so you must do what works for you. Sometimes it pays you to just *'be'* rather than *'do'*, so whatever helps you achieve this state, will give you the space to open up new thinking. Conversely, anything that has the reverse effect and becomes an energy drainer, you need to turn round to negate the impact e.g. too much isolation can often create negative thinking and mindset, which is often one of the biggest causes of procrastination.

✎ *Exercise – Recruit Yourself and Winning with Attitude*

Reviewing your Skills, Motivated Abilities and Attributes from previous exercises, consider which are your top ten Skills and Attributes/Attitudinal aspects which will make the difference to achieving your next job or change of career and life goals. You can use these for self marketing and to focus your energy to bring about your desired outcomes.

	Attitudes/Attributes	Skills
1		
2		
3		
4		
5		

6		
7		
8		
9		
10		

The Power And Value Of Social Media

The Growth Of Social Media

With the growth of Social Media has come the importance of having an online brand and presence. A good online profile or bio can make all the difference to you being found by the right people. The power of Social Media is the fact that you can talk to *so many people so quickly* when to do so face to face would take weeks and months. Everyone needs to embrace Social Media as the most effective form of communication, whether you are running your own business or whether you are a serious professional in your specific business sector.

LinkedIn

LinkedIn (www.linkedin.com) is the professional version of Facebook. Although there are numerous imitations, LinkedIn is accepted as **the place** where professional people meet. As I write, it is estimated there are now 35 million users with a new member joining every two minutes! You could say it is rather like a market place or shopping mall where you can have access to a huge number of potential connections and information to help you in your career quest. Therefore, use LinkedIn as your main business social network to develop your profile, online brand and presence, so you can be found and you can find and network with others. Getting quality recommendations for your profile and likewise giving quality recommendations for your valued and trusted connections can give you kudos and help you stand out from the crowd.

LinkedIn has literally hundreds if not thousands of different online groups related to a huge variety of different sectors and business disciplines. These groups are a great way to learn about the latest trends, share knowledge and experience and develop your network with like minded people. By getting involved in the many discussion forums, you also have a great opportunity to position yourself as an expert. Raising your profile in this way, will prompt people to look at your profile and, if they like what they see, they could well contact you to connect or possibly regarding potential jobs or self employed opportunities.

If you are looking at a career change, explore the different types of groups in your field of interest before you decide which ones to join. Sometimes people put postings on such groups asking for thoughts on the best way to transition into this sector. Again, this is an excellent way to show that you are in the market and get your name across and be noticed.

It is important to embrace the technological changes that are happening around us and LinkedIn is likely to be one of the most important to you, regardless of whether you wish to be employed or self employed. By ignoring LinkedIn you do so at your peril, as you are cutting off one of the most important community and communication channels. Follow the adage 'you need to be in it to win it'. If you are concerned about how to set up your profile or get the best out of LinkedIn and this is holding you back, you can find numerous video tutorials on YouTube plus tutorials on LinkedIn itself and other websites and blogs. This is another opportunity where you can seek help from family, friends or utilise your networks of contacts who are already using the site effectively.

Facebook

Although most people associate Facebook (www.facebook.com) with purely personal social activity, the general networking principle is wonderfully illustrated by a woman who attended one of my workshops a couple of years ago. Having explained the importance of both offline and online networking and the power of social media, she declared that her best friend had just got her most recent job through Facebook! I noticed the quizzical looks from the other delegates, so asked her to explain to the group how her friend had achieved this.

It transpired that her friend had messaged out to her friends on Facebook, stating 'she was between jobs and exploring new opportunities in her particular field and did anyone know of any contacts they could put her in touch with?' She received two responses, one of whom invited her to a meeting and she got the job straightaway. The timescale - only two weeks from start to finish! Compare this with the average job application, which can take anything from one month to well over three months.

What this woman did was no different to phoning or meeting with a number of close contacts to achieve the same goal. However, the difference was in the speed of the whole process, which cannot be understated. This is the power of using your networks on Social Media. It is not just about reaching out to your connections; it is their connections that may help to unlock the key to your future. Equally importantly, she also bypassed the traditional recruitment process, which we will look at shortly.

Be careful how you manage your reputation on Facebook

One of my clients, a company director, shared a story with me about one of their employees, who worked with mainly black and minority ethnic colleagues and who had his Facebook page plastered with politically incorrect images and racist comments. Identified as a disaster waiting to happen, he was duly sacked.

Unwittingly some people may choose to post 'racy' photos on their Facebook pages and, although these might be considered by some to be fun at the time, potential employers can access these when investigating potential candidates simply by using any search engine, such as Google. Unless you are going into modelling, keep such photos and your Facebook status 'private', so only your personal connections can see them otherwise you are asking for trouble. The same applies to people who inadvertently show drunken exploits to the world. There have even been cases of employees taking a 'sickie' and then posting about their hangover on Facebook and subsequently getting sacked! Make sure only the people you want to see these can, or seriously consider whether you should have them on Facebook at all.

Twitter

Unless you have become an avid tweeter, you are unlikely to know what all the fuss is about and why Twitter (https://twitter.com) has become an integral part of many people's daily lives. Apart from the main use for quick fire instant messages of maximum 140 characters and general chit chat, Twitter has become a useful search engine tool in its own right and with the likes of www.twitjobsearch.com rapidly becoming the way many people now search for job vacancies. In addition, the main benefit of Twitter is as yet another way for you to build your online presence and personal or company brand, when you use it as a marketing tool. Using Twitter as a way to develop your personal brand can be very effective if you decide to start your own business. You can quickly open up new communication channels, participate in conversations and send regular 'micro blogs', which in turn will help you develop a new community to position you as an expert in your chosen field. As Twitter is a global social media tool, as with LinkedIn, by using it tactically and sharing lots of useful nuggets of information, it could open up unexpected new opportunities. One thing is certain, Twitter will evolve and change in ways that you should aim to keep abreast of, so if you don't get involved now, keep an open mind when you relaunch your career.

Blogs

Whereas Twitter is focused on short, sharp blasts of specific, often daily or more regular communications, a blog is basically a journal that is available on the web. It can be anything from daily to ad hoc regularity. You need not concern yourself with setting up a blog at this stage, unless you love writing, are planning to start your own business, or want to blog as part of a portfolio career. Blogs are more like personalised web sites where you use 'your voice' (or your business voice) to share knowledge, expertise and interesting information to get you or your business noticed. Blogs are also an excellent way of positioning you, as a thought leader in your area of specialism or interest and therefore for building your personal or business brand.

Networking

In my experience, the biggest fears facing people who experience redundancy are:

- Networking
- Understanding how to find new opportunities
- Establishing strategies to tap into the 'hidden job market'

Interestingly, most people I come across are already doing some form of networking without realising it, either internally or externally within their organisations almost every day of their employed lives. You may go to conferences and seminars, meet with external suppliers or third party agencies, all of which becomes part of your working life and you take for granted as part of your job. After redundancy many people psychologically see networking differently. It seems to take on a whole new negative meaning because they are now seeking help to find a new job or opportunities. But this is yet another limiting belief and perception, because in reality there is little difference - they are still just conversations over a cup of coffee!

What networking is?

Networking is all about making connections and building business relationships which is exactly the same as you would in any employed role. Just as you would share knowledge and information with your networks when employed, you can do the same whilst you're exploring opportunities. Yet again, this is all about changing your mindset.

What networking isn't?

The biggest mistake most people make when starting out on personal networking, to explore opportunities, is the 'give us a job syndrome'. I've seen so many people frighten away potential useful connections because of their overly aggressive approach asking people outright if they have any jobs suitable for them. What should you do? One of the key principles of networking is to view every person you speak to online or offline, as someone who can introduce you to one or two other contacts who may know someone who can help you or move you one step closer to your desired goal. You should be constantly looking for information and new connections to move you forward.

Networking is also a two way process and **givers gain**. Therefore, one good deed deserves another so always establish how you might be able to help the other person in any networking conversations and communications. Whilst you are networking, listening is often more powerful than talking, whether online or offline. You might think there is no way you could help anybody else but if you don't ask you will never know. The most successful networkers are always those who think of others first. I'm sure you would like to be thought of in this light too, wouldn't you?

Crystallising a need

I've come across many wonderful examples of my clients who have embraced networking in a very targeted and specific way to achieve their career goals. By networking and being introduced, referred or recommended to a potential employer through key and influential contacts, can make a huge difference to your success.

It is not always the case that a company has made a decision to recruit an addition to their team. As with many things in life, timing can be all important. Sometimes by being in the right place at the right time you could be the person to crystallise a need they may have been considering but had not formalised.

Below are some wonderful examples of how tapping into different types of networking connections can pay real dividends. Please note the same applies equally as importantly if you are running your own business, self employed or looking for any type of contract, project or business opportunity.

📖 *Les's Story*

This is probably the most amazing networking story of the hundreds I could share with you but for the most unexpected reason. Everything was going right for Les, having landed a great job in Silicon Valley, California during the boom time for the IT industry. He married an American woman and was looking forward to developing his career and life in California. Unfortunately, the rug was pulled and with no job he had to return to the UK with his wife. This coincided with the .com bust and it was a really difficult time to find high level IT jobs. Les was adamant that having been away from the UK for a number of years he had exhausted his networks. Having heard similar stories numerous times, I have never been convinced that this is true. I continued to encourage him to explore and develop new networks, constantly reminding him to target different categories of people.

I always remember when he shared his amazing story. He was beaming when we met, saying he had some exciting news to share. I thought he must have finally secured a job after many months of trying. I was close, but was not prepared for what he did say when he admitted he had not been totally honest with me regarding his networks. Unbelievably, he had not told his lifelong best friend, who had flown out to the States to be best man at his wedding, of his true situation i.e. being unemployed and on benefits!

He finally took the bull by the horns and invited his best mate out for a beer and after a couple of pints, plucked up the courage to tell the truth. I'm sure you can imagine the reaction of his best friend, which was prefaced by a number of expletives *'idiot, why didn't you tell me?'* Les explained he was too embarrassed to admit he was out of work and therefore fabricated different consultancy roles instead. His friend, being a lawyer, had a huge range of contacts. After his initial shock, he promised to come back to Les with details of one of his clients, the MD of a software company.

To cut a very long story short, they met and he was offered the option of a short term contract with the possibility to review, based on the success of the project and the improvement in the financial situation of the company. Les decided to go for an alternative option of doing the project work on a freelance basis. This way it gave him more flexibility, a quick get out if the company's financial situation didn't improve and renewed confidence to look at this project to open up new opportunities moving forward. They agreed terms and it became the start of him running his own IT consultancy, which I had encouraged him to do for months. Goodness knows what would have happened had he never told his best friend!

Key learning points for Networking:

- Networking does not need to be scary
- Networking is a great skill to learn and hone both online and offline
- Networking is not just about you – it is a 2 way process – **givers gain!**
- Focus on gaining recommended contacts and useful information
- Networking helps to identify opportunities

- Networking creates opportunities
- Networking helps you tap into the hidden job market
- Most people genuinely want to help you
- You never know who may unlock the key to your future

Most importantly, don't follow the 'herd'. Instead, bypass the competition and recruitment process (if looking for a job) by networking yourself into situations where you ideally get introduced, referred or recommended, so you are ahead of the game!

NETWORKING - AIM TO CONNECT

PROFESSIONAL ASSOCIATIONS
THE COMMUNITY
SUPPLIERS
EX BOSSES
EX WORK COLLEAGUES
FAMILY & FRIENDS
YOU

So, how do you go about developing and optimising your networks?

If you are new to networking or you are a reluctant networker, as I was initially following my redundancy, the following approach will go a long way to break down your barriers and get you started. Once you get into the swing of networking, you like me, will never look back and it will become a part of your everyday business life.

The image depicts a simple but highly effective networking approach I developed a number of years ago, which I call the 'reverse target' approach. *Why reverse target?* Because you would normally aim at the bulls eye at the middle of the target, wouldn't you? Instead, taking this approach will help you build your networking confidence and ability, because you start within your comfort zone, talking with family and friends. The key is to focus on asking people who they know and who has contacts in the field you are interested in, or who might have knowledge that could steer you in the right direction. As you gain in confidence, you can then work outwards as each category is likely to seem less daunting. The 'Community' can be any contacts in groups or clubs you belong to e.g. religious, political, hobbies, sports, leisure, your gym etc. Since establishing commonality is one of the most helpful aspects of networking, it should always be easier when you are talking with like minded people, which you will have seen from the case studies highlighted.

As you gradually move outwards, reaching new targets, you will be gaining new contacts all the time. It is important to understand that it is not just about the initial contacts you make and how you build rapport and relationships with them. You now have an opportunity to develop your networks even further by tapping into other people's contacts as well, which will help you reach a contact currently out of your own circles. This is where networking becomes very powerful and is the principle on which all the Social Media networks such as Facebook and LinkedIn are built, because you never know who it might be possible to connect with and where this might lead you. Remember, you never know who will unlock the key to your future. It will probably be someone you actually don't know right now.

✎ *Exercise – Expanding Your Network*

Following the principles highlighted in the last section, use the example below to create your own spreadsheet or table and highlight people you would ideally like to contact, or definitely need to contact in order to add to your network. Also indicate the best method to contact each person online or offline (i.e. via LinkedIn, Facebook, email or by telephone). You can then prioritise your list and add timescales to ensure you have a target to keep you focused.

Network Category	New Contacts	Method To Connect
Family and friends		
Ex work colleagues		

Ex boss		
Suppliers		
Leisure & community		
Professional associations		

The Hidden Job Market

You may have heard this term before but not understood the importance. The 'hidden job market' is the chunk of the job market, which as it implies, is hidden from view from most people. What do I mean by 'hidden'; quite simply these jobs are not advertised in the public domain, e.g. national press, regional or local press, company websites or recruitment agencies.

What is the size of the hidden Job Market?

I always ask my clients this question to check their knowledge and understanding. What do you think? Most people say around 20% of jobs would not be advertised. If you believe this then you are in for one hell of a shock! Over the last decade, career researchers and commentators have suggested that between 60% to 80% of all jobs are never advertised in the public domain! For management roles, the view is around 80% as the norm. These figures also tend to increase during recession and times of economic uncertainty, as we are experiencing now.

So where are the jobs?

It is often the case that an employer has a need to recruit but due to cost controls has a ban on recruitment advertising. To overcome the inability to advertise, many private sector employers may just source new staff through their own employees. 'Introduce a friend' schemes, where employers pay a fee to the introducing employee once the new recruit has passed any probationary period, are increasingly common.

Why do they do this? Quite simply it is good economics. Existing employees are unlikely to introduce anybody except good candidates because their own reputation is at stake. Employers' 'bounties' can be anything from a couple of hundred pounds to a couple of thousand pounds depending on the sector and the level of the job role. This may seem a lot of money but compared to typical recruitment agency rates e.g. anything from 10% to 40% of annual salary, this is a massive cost saving.

In the current economic climate, many employers are reluctant to use recruitment agencies and executive search companies, except for the most prestigious roles. If we look at a typical middle management role at circa £40,000, an employer could be paying a recruitment agency an average fee of £8000 if at 20% of salary. You can now see why paying existing employees to introduce a friend could be massively cost and time saving to the company.

How do you tap into the hidden Job Market?

In today's rapidly changing marketplace, many job vacancies are only advertised via sector specific groups on LinkedIn, e.g. the largest being HR, Marketing, Finance and IT. If you are not signed up to some of these groups and you are looking for opportunities in these and other sectors, you are very likely to miss out. You have to be in it to win it, as I have said before! Other key ways to tap into this market are by following the strategies highlighted in this Chapter e.g. targeted speculative applications, being opportunistic, developing relationships with selected head hunters (who may have exclusivity to recruit) and above all else, effective networking and use of Social Media. I cannot stress enough that you ignore these strategies at your peril!

Portfolio Career Options – Turning Talents And Passions Into Profit!

A Lifestyle Choice

This brings us back to Portfolio Careers. As in my case and for many of my clients, friends and contacts, try forgetting the whole concept of *"A job"* – instead reframe the job concept altogether so that *"It's not about a job or a career necessarily anymore, it's about generating income in a way that meets all your lifestyle objectives"*, which will come from your re-evaluation and income objectives in Chapter two.

Developing a portfolio career means seeking fulfilment from tapping into your true marketability in terms of your skills, natural talents, attributes, passions and interests. By tapping into your connections, you may open up opportunities for potential collaborations with like minded people whilst keeping your contacts informed of what you are now offering.

For many people developing a Portfolio Career is also a key lifestyle choice. It is about reshaping your career and redesigning your life. Charles Handy originally coined the term "Portfolio Life" in his book '*The Age of Unreason*' in 1989. He describes a portfolio life as *"a portfolio of activities – some we do for money, some for interest, some for pleasure, some for a cause…the different bits fit together to form a balanced whole…greater than the parts"*.

I remember vividly extolling the virtues of a portfolio career to a group of unemployed professionals and executives a number of years ago. One of my delegates leapt out of his chair and punched the air and exclaimed. I wondered what on earth he was doing! Like many people, he had not been able to see past getting another job. However, the realisation that a portfolio career could encompass a mix of voluntary work, self employed work plus even part time employed work really excited him. His view was that he would even push trolleys in a supermarket car park a few days a week, if it gave him the flexibility and CHOICE he was looking for. He wanted to develop his business idea, but still needed some income and he wanted to continue his voluntary work one day a week. This was a real 'eureka moment' for him and he was already seeing the possibilities, which was brilliant.

How Can A Portfolio Lifestyle Work For You? – Your Opportunity To Reflect

Mindful of Charles Handy's definition above, let's take a closer look at a 'Portfolio Lifestyle' and how it can work for ***you***:

"Like the sections of a colourful umbrella, you choose from your selection of strengths, skills and talents to best suit you and your clients. Each segment provides you with an opportunity to challenge, to motivate and to grow. With a firm grip on your umbrella, you hold your portfolio life together and it provides a canopy of choice."

Gail Gibson, 2011

It was Gail's fascinating description of a portfolio career and lifestyle, on a LinkedIn group, that so resonated with me and attracted my attention. It was very apparent there were some real synergies between us by the way we shared similar thinking in the group, so we met. The result was developing our *'How Colourful is Your Umbrella - Creating Your Portfolio of Choice'* Portfolio Career and Lifestyle concept. We now run seminars, Masterclasses, have published a 2 CD / MP3 set audio book and are planning to co-author a mainstream book. Much of this information is available on my Career Catalyst website link: **http://www.steveprestonthecareercatalyst.com/index.php/masterclasses/14-how-colourful-is-your-umbrella**

What we have achieved is an excellent example of a mutually beneficial collaboration with a like minded person, with shared values and beliefs, who has also become a valued and trusted friend. It doesn't get much better than that, does it?

A successful portfolio life is a curious and self fulfilling mix of challenge, diversity and inspiration. This alternative way of thinking, working and living provides you with an opportunity to embrace choice, freedom and purpose. A portfolio life allows you to step aside from conventional, conditioned thinking around the "need to get another job".

Perhaps the greatest aspect of this working lifestyle is that you can choose who you work with, how you work with them, when you work and where you work. You have the flexibility to add and change the strands to 'your colourful umbrella' and for it to transform into '**your** portfolio of CHOICE!'

I remember many years ago being impressed by an Interim HR Director who worked 4 days a week and on Fridays taught in a school. It was something she loved and it was also a commitment to a close friend. She really valued her teaching job and saw this as a mutually beneficial situation, a key part of her life and around which she planned everything else. We will look more closely at Interim Management in Chapter five.

Top tip to make your portfolio career work for you

One of the best pieces of advice I have ever been given in relation to portfolio careers, is to find one strand of work that can pretty much guarantee regular work, which will help to cover most of your bills, then develop other strands alongside it. This makes perfect sense and also helps to reduce yet another 'fear factor 'or limiting belief that you won't make it work.

How will you define your working lifestyle into the future?

What if you were to say, "*I choose to build a working lifestyle based on what I love to do and what I am good at*". Think about it. You give yourself an opportunity to start a new career path for yourself, one that is built on passion, talent and belief. You give yourself an opportunity to step away from the uncertainty of needing to have a job and you can almost bypass the possibility of losing your job again as well. In effect you have a golden opportunity to attempt to 'future proof' what you do. You have the power to reshape your career and create a more robust framework to allow you to redesign your life! When I came across these profound quotes from Peter Drucker, the renowned business guru, over a decade ago, they really made me sit up and take notice and radically changed my views on work and life: *"Corporations once built to last like pyramids are now more like tents... You can't design your life around a temporary structure."* Harvard Business Review, May1993. How amazingly perceptive he was and things have only got worse since! The Portfolio lifestyle is an amazing and life changing concept. It is not for everyone but if it sounds enticing, what do you have to lose?

Keep building your momentum

Are you thinking: So many questions, yet not enough answers? Remember the key is to focus on your target. Keep building momentum and tackle everything in manageable chunks. Just as we covered in Chapter one, the area of mindset is absolutely massive and it is wise to consider this piecemeal. From my experience, the people who tend to make the quickest breakthroughs and fastest transformations are those who have planned and whose mindset is very strong. If you are determined not to get derailed and can accept that it is in the nature of the career transition and Cycle process that you might move two steps forward and one step back, then providing you have the right attitude, determination and belief in the process and keep following it, you will ultimately succeed.

Summary

With your jigsaw pieces coming together you can now start developing a laser focus aimed at your future targets.

Here are the key conclusions from Step 4 of the process:

- Be bold - It is never too late to realise aspirations you have always wanted to achieve but never been brave enough or had the time to try
- Follow your passions and you will find a way to make things happen for you
- Don't jump out of the frying pan and into the fire!
- A job is good but it might not be great or the right answer for you
- Research and networking are key to exploring and opening up new opportunities
- Set your sights high and step out of your comfort zone to create real opportunities
- Listen to your Inner voice and follow your gut feelings - they are usually right
- You don't have to continue work you don't really enjoy, even if you are good at it
- Be true to yourself and your values and you will be happy
- The Law of Attraction is powerful so focus on your intent and what you want more of
- Now is the time to develop a compelling CV, bios and online profiles

- Learn to love Social Media, especially LinkedIn and develop your online brand and presence to make it work for you
- Take care to manage your online reputation, especially on Facebook
- Keep an open mind - If your ***WHY*** is strong enough the ***WHAT*** and ***HOW*** will follow
- Volunteering or work shadowing are great ways to try something new to see if it's right for you
- Give yourself 'permission' to face your fears head on and banish them, especially about networking!
- Don't let procrastination rule - Find the best way for you to spend productive days
- Learn to be opportunistic and you may crystallise a need
- Network your way to tap into the 'hidden job market' and circumnavigate the recruitment process
- A portfolio career and turning your talents and passions into generating the income and lifestyle you want is a whole new world of opportunity and fulfilling option
- It's your future - Don't let other people control it. Take control yourself and learn to become 'the architect of your own future'!
- With the right mindset, belief and actions you can achieve almost anything!

Congratulations, you are now ready to move quickly onto **Step 5 - 'Deciding what to do'!**

CHAPTER 5

Deciding What To Do – Step 5

"What we can or cannot do, what we consider possible or impossible is rarely a function of our true capability. It is more likely a function of our beliefs about who we are"

Anthony Robbins

Having started down the path of researching, networking and exploring opportunities, this step of the Cycle is about coming to the right conclusion about what you want to do next. The only thing that can hold you back now is your own fears or limiting beliefs about what is possible. This Chapter also includes practical strategies for taking the next step. It may be that an interest outside work or a previously untapped area of your skills and knowledge has the potential to become a temporary income stream, even form part of a portfolio career or become your new business offering.

Depending on how focused or seriously you have worked on your career transition so far, you now need to take full responsibility, in order to decide what to do and achieve a successful outcome. If you have not done so already, start thinking much more clearly about short, medium and longer term goals. You might decide to get another job, as your immediate priority, but know that your ultimate goal is to start your own business or develop a portfolio career. So you may find at this stage that there is a lot of clutter to work through and the array of considerations can grow like 'weeds' that become entangled and can choke your 'new shoots of growth' unless they are tended and the weeds removed. Whatever your current mindset, only **you** can now make things happen to achieve your desired end goal.

The Career 'Trap'

How Did You Choose A Career Or Actually Decide What Work To Do?

You may be reflecting on this question. My experience is that unless you set out with the specific intention of being a doctor, lawyer, nurse, dentist, engineer or other profession and went to university to study for such careers, for the majority of people it was more about luck, chance, peer pressure, parental and teacher influences or just falling into jobs. My thoughts are substantiated by conversations with clients, friends, close contacts and discussions in online forums.

As a result, you don't necessarily have a career plan but develop your career by working for a specific company for a while, get promoted and grow your career within that company. You then move on, doing similar work in another company and before you know where you are you have unwittingly entered the 'Career Trap' and become ensnared. What tends to happen for many people is that they just roll on in the same old way following a linear career path. Suddenly, they reach the point of no return because they are fed up and want to change or the rug is pulled from under them, like now. I'm sure this sounds like a familiar story.

The CHOICE Now Is To Do Something Different And Reinvent Yourself

For those of you who've had long careers, you will find there are so many more opportunities to change into new and different careers than when you first set out. With the advent and phenomenal growth of the Internet, there are now multitudes of different ways to earn a living, which would have previously been inconceivable. We will look at a range of possible options in this Chapter. The difference now, is you do have the CHOICE and the chance to plan and become the architect of your own future to create the work and lifestyle you want.

It is my experience at this stage of the Career Navigation Cycle process that you will now either be flying and ready to make key decisions about what you wish to do next, or you might still be confused and need to untangle some weeds in your mind. What do I mean by this? Consider carefully what is stopping you from making the decision about what to do next? Having provided you with all the strategies you need to explore opportunities in Chapter four, realistically, the only thing that can be holding you back is you.

If so, ask yourself:

- Are you still unsure whether you wish to be employed or self employed?
- Do you doubt your ability to run your own business?
- Are you still unclear on what it is you can do next?
- Do you doubt your ability to make a successful career change?

Some of your answers may still be limiting beliefs which you need to challenge. Read on and see where this leads you.

Health Warning...

Bear in mind that at this step of the Cycle you are likely to journey back and forth to step 4 and maybe even Steps 2 and 3 in order to clarify your thinking. You should not view this as negative or that you are not making progress. Accept it as a natural part of your journey and the career transition process, as you narrow down your thinking and make key decisions about what to do.

Moving From Chaos To Clarity

Untangle The Weeds In Your Mind

A garden entangled and enmeshed with weeds can only give rise to 'chaos' and yet some simple tidying will allow you to see the path and gain 'clarity'. Likewise, at this stage of the Cycle, as you move through your voyage of self discovery to reach your next destination, it is important to do a spot of metaphorical gardening and some 'weeding of the mind'.

The acronyms below demonstrate the typical emotions and feelings experienced during this journey **from CHAOS to CLARITY.** How many of these resonate with you?

FROM CHAOS COMES CLARITY

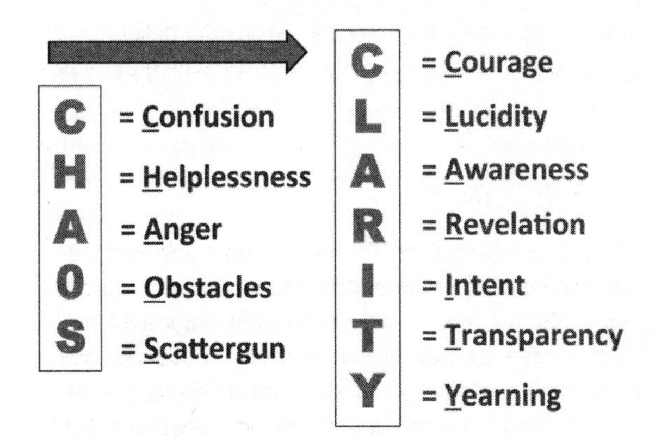

If you're still struggling to find the lucidity, your revelation and your intent is not yet transparent, you will almost certainly find the answers by rereading some of the earlier Chapters and reviewing the work you have done from the many exercises in the book. I guarantee the answers will either be staring you in the face or they are hidden because you may still have some limiting beliefs to overcome first. Don't forget, you are still on an emotional roller coaster and you may have some twists and turns to manoeuvre before you head on the upswing towards your new life path.

The Thief Of Time

"Time is what we want most, but what we use worst."

William Penn, Founder of the Province of Pennsylvania, USA, 1644 -1718

This poignant quote became so reminiscent of my own situation following redundancy, when I often felt time was both a blessing and a curse. I realise now that this was no more than a transition and that timescales for such a journey can vary depending upon an individual's personal circumstances. Some say that procrastination is the thief of time, but I now say this needs to be balanced with a degree of patience and planning. As I have explained during the previous Chapters, the early stages of redundancy will give rise to a whole roller coaster of emotions and reactions, but time moves on and sometimes it feels as though it has passed all too quickly. We will now explore a number of ways in which you can make time work for you. First, let's examine the impact time can have as the months fly past.

Hitting The 'Six Month Psychological Time Barrier'

Society (and Job Centre Plus) conditions us to believe that if you haven't achieved job success by six months after redundancy you have failed. Therefore, the six month mark becomes your 'wake-up call'. The fact that my transition took me a year is living proof that this is not true at all and I've worked with hundreds of clients for whom it took much longer than six months. Depending on your situation, how badly you have been affected by your redundancy and what support networks you have, it can take you fully six months to even 'let go and look forward'.

As I've stated from the outset, you are on a journey and there is no set time to make your career transition. Everyone will have different motivations and timescales. What often happens is that you start off down the road thinking you will get another job and as time goes by, as part of your ongoing re-evaluation, the more work you do on yourself and the more self aware you become, you start to think:

- Maybe there are other options after all?
- You don't really want to work for anyone else anymore
- You have had it applying for lots of jobs without success
- Maybe you can set up a business of your own?

Remember *Ben Sweetland's quote "Success is a journey not a destination".*

Now Is The Time To Get Serious!

From my experience you will find the time will fly following redundancy (although the days may seem long) and six months can easily pass before you know it. I've met many people over the years, especially highflying professionals and executives, who made a conscious decision to spend valuable time with their families during their transition period, especially if they had young children. This is time that you will never be able to replace once you're back in employment or running your own business, so it is a very personal short term decision.

A word of caution, it may be right for you to take some time out for all manner of reasons, depending on your personal situation. However, it is imperative that you do get serious and focused before your money starts to run out. Although I have met a few people over the years who managed to just 'flick the switch on' and move into serious job search mode and secure a job, these are the exception rather than the rule. My experience is that for the majority of people, the longer you're out of work the harder it is to get back into the work mindset. Bear this in mind so you can ramp up your 'campaign' to get serious and achieve your laser focus, which you will need to start achieving the results you want. Regardless of your situation, the six month milestone is another excellent time to review, take stock and refocus. If you haven't done so already, now is the time to start some serious action planning, which we will look at in Chapter six.

Time To Step Out Of Your Comfort Zone

Sometimes, at this stage of the Cycle you can lose focus and may get distracted. Alternatively, you might be raring to go in order to determine what you want to do next. This can be both exciting and scary. Procrastination is the killer for a huge percentage of people during the career transition process. I can certainly put up my hand and honestly say that was the case with me. This also relates back to the question of the six month psychological barrier, as often it's procrastination that causes that problem. Deciding what to do for a lot of people is scary because, having completed your research and explored opportunities, the realisation could be that your passions, interests, true marketability and values are all providing evidence for you, which now needs decisions. However, only **you** can take the responsibility for your success and make anything happen. For some people this will take them well outside their comfort zone but for others, it will become the 'thrill of the chase'!

One of the most important things I've learnt, as an expert in career and personal development, is that you don't achieve anything worthwhile in your life without coming out of your comfort zone. As long as you understand this, are prepared to work at it, then you will get the ultimate reward of finding a job, career or work you love, so you can lead a fulfilling life. We will revisit stretching out of your comfort zone in more detail in Chapter six.

Take Time To Get Any Additional Support You May Need

If you really are stuck at this point, it will definitely pay you to get support from a Career Coach, Mentor or Adviser who can add real value to help you turn your ideas into reality. What support you need depends on what your decisions are at this stage. For example, if you decide to set up a specific type of business and would feel more confident working with someone who has already done it, your best bet would be to find a suitable mentor. A good example, is a client I was working with a few years ago, who was recommended to me because he wanted to break free from the shackles of The National Health Service and explore a career change:

Malcolm's Story

Malcolm wanted to understand how he could use his undoubted skills, attributes and passions to do something different that would be of interest to him in the latter stages of his career and provide him with a sense of purpose and fulfilment. I coached him through a few sessions round the Cycle to Step 4, where one option he was considering was setting up his own consultancy to do work in the Health Service and Charity sectors. At this point, I networked him to a contact of mine, who had already trodden this same path. Whereas, I would have continued to coach him to reach definite conclusions, by taking this approach he had the benefit of an industry specialist who was able to share her knowledge and experience and act as a mentor for Malcolm. Having such a valued and trusted mentor gave him a head start and was also a great boost to his confidence, to follow a similar path.

Health Warning...

Before you engage any additional support, just as you would with a builder or electrician, make sure the person you choose comes highly recommended. This is a key investment in your time and money, so it is important you have the right chemistry with your coach, mentor or adviser. Unfortunately there are plenty of people who will take your money without a thought, so always check for valid testimonials plus accreditations from relevant professional associations e.g. Association for Coaching or Institute of Leadership and Management.

The Financial Implication Of Time Passing

If you're in the unfortunate situation of having completed your financial re-evaluation and know your money is going to run out at or before six months, it's understandable that you might go into panic mode and want to take the first job that comes along. However, try to think of job searching like taking photographs. You think you have found the ideal picture but before you know it an even better picture comes along right afterwards. It's similar with job offers. It is also amazing how often you get your first job offer and then another comes along, just like buses all seem to come at the same time!

This is why being hasty and taking the first job offer is one of the things you should try to avoid. Of course this would not be the case if the job was a great fit and met the majority of your values and needs. Just be aware of not making too many compromises. Whichever way you look at it, being out of work for six months is a key milestone and psychological barrier and only you will know whether you now have to up your game, have a total rethink or start your real work, if you have taken time out.

If you are signed on at Jobcentre Plus, the six month milestone is also a key review point for Jobseekers Allowance, any other benefits you may be claiming and also funded training opportunities. Ironically, the time when you might need additional support, direction and a confidence boost, is the time when they tend to put you under the most pressure. Therefore, you need to weigh up the pros and cons of continuing to sign on. Do any financial or training benefits outweigh the demoralising aspects of this unpleasant experience? If so, fine, if not, you should be guided by your inner voice and gut feelings, rather than your pride.

As with any government policies the rules regarding benefits and training opportunities are constantly changing so it is important you keep abreast of what you are entitled to. I must stress again, there is no one size fits all and your situation could be very different to other people you know who have also been affected by redundancy. If you have decided to take a few months out to go travelling or undertake certain projects around the house, then clearly this six month milestone will have completely different implications than if you have been constantly job searching and soul searching from day one post your redundancy. Regardless, keep following and believing in the Career Navigation Cycle process and enjoy your journey.

The Universal Laws Of Success And Achievement

Why Are Some People More Successful Than Others?

I have made various mentions of Brian Tracy in the earlier Chapters of the book. A remarkable psychologist, author and speaker, he has dedicated much of his life to studying Universal Laws of Success and Achievement, some dating back to Aristotle. These revelations can be life changing for you, too, as success is not a miracle, an accident nor is it a matter of luck. There are many universal laws which affect success, and understanding these laws puts a completely different perspective on life. Let's now consider three such laws:

(i) The Law of Cause and Effect: Everything happens for a reason; for every effect there is a specific cause

Aristotle asserted that we live in a world governed by law, not chance. He stated that everything happens for a reason, whether or not we know what it is. He said that every effect has a specific cause or causes. Every cause or action has an effect of some kind or another, whether we can see it and whether we like it or not. This law says that achievement, wealth, happiness, prosperity and business success are all the direct and indirect effects or results of specific causes or actions. This simply means that, if you can be clear about the effect or result you want, you can probably achieve it. Also, by studying others who have achieved the same goal to which you aspire e.g. starting up your own business or achieving financial independence, **by replicating the actions they took**, you in turn can achieve the same results.

(ii) The Law of Attraction

You are a living magnet; you invariably attract into your life the people, situations and circumstances that are in harmony with your dominant thoughts. The Law of Attraction states that our thinking creates and brings to us whatever we think about. In essence this means that like attracts like and that by focusing on positive or negative thoughts, one can bring about positive or negative results.

This is the emphasis of The Law of Attraction, which we first started exploring in Chapter one and we revisited in Chapter four, where we explored the importance of focusing on what you want and your intent. In Chapter one, I explained the importance of your mindset. At this stage of the Cycle and career transition process, having a positive mindset becomes ever more important. For instance:

(a) If your thinking has always been and still is *"I can't see myself in a new role and I know I'm going to be in the same position in 6 months' time"*, then this is exactly what is likely to manifest, as you are focusing your energy on what you don't want.

(b) Conversely, if your focus and thinking is and has been *"I will have made my career change within six months into a new career and work I love"*, then this is more than likely what will happen.

Isn't it good to see the difference in these two statements and the switch to focusing on what you do want with positive energy? By taking this approach you will take control of your career to become the architect of your own future in the timescale that works for you.

(iii) The Law of Requisite Variety

I discovered the Law of Requisite Variety when working with one of my clients who is an NLP (Neuro Linguistic Programming) practitioner. This law is taken from the field of cybernetics, which in laymen's terms proves that if something that you are doing isn't producing results, do something else. If what you're doing isn't working then 'something else' has much more chance of success, as there are always alternatives. In these circumstances you can carry on doing the same things and continue to produce unwanted results, or you can adapt your behaviour as necessary until you get your desired outcome. This might be considered 'common sense', so you don't want to be one of these people trying to beat their head against a brick wall, do you?

Your Career Options

The world of work has changed over the past few decades. New technology, especially the Internet and mobile technology, has radically changed the way we work. If you've had a long career in one sector, it is highly likely you will be oblivious to the wealth of new career and work options now available. In today's online, digital 24/7 environment of the 'information and knowledge worker', pretty much anything is possible, regardless of your age. You certainly won't be short of options, which in itself can be both exciting and scary. Either way, I'm sure you will agree this is great cause for encouragement, as you do have CHOICE!

I have challenged you throughout this book to consider whether you wish to be employed or self employed or maybe even develop a portfolio career and lifestyle. However, there are still multiple opportunities within self employed and portfolio career options. Before you come to any definite conclusions, let's now look at a range of options which you may have never previously considered, including some web and home based businesses. This is just a small sample, so to find out more, you will need to continue with your research, just as in Step 4. Opportunities to earn money from the web are far too numerous to mention. However, I have highlighted a couple of interesting examples which involve little or no investment, minimal training and are becoming increasingly popular due to the quick turnaround time to be able to trade.

Consulting

What is consulting?

Consulting is becoming an increasingly broader industry, incorporating roles such as management consultants, IT consultants, recruitment consultants, business advisers, training consultants, HR consultants, marketing and media consultants to name just a few. Whichever way you look at it consultancy is a varied profession, with projects and clients changing constantly. This can be the beauty but also the challenge of this profession.

Definition of consulting

"The provision to businesses of objective advice and assistance relating to the strategy, structure, management and operations of an organisation in pursuit of its long term purposes and objectives. Such assistance may include the identification of options with recommendations; the provision of additional resources; and/or the implementation of solutions."

The Institute of Consulting

In a nutshell, a consultant provides external advice for organisations that require specialist expertise or an objective outside perspective on their business. For many professionals, following redundancy, if you are an expert in your field, consulting is an obvious, sensible route and a reasonably 'safe' option, just as it was with me when I started my own business.

What makes a successful consultant?

- You are well respected for your knowledge and expertise in your sector
- You always work to high professional standards
- You have developed a good network with many valued and trusted connections
- You are a strategic thinker good at seeing the bigger picture
- You have excellent communication skills with the ability to highlight key information either in written reports or verbally, to enable stakeholders or key decision makers to take action

- You are able to work well at all levels of the organisation, especially with senior executives and the Board
- You have a strong personal brand and project an air of confidence and self belief
- If you don't know the answer you know someone who does and can collaborate with them to achieve your desired goal
- You can sell and market yourself effectively
- You can use previous projects to highlight your competency whilst being mindful of confidentiality

Does this sound like you? If so, consulting could be an option.

Interim Management

In the current economic climate, Interim Management is becoming increasingly important in the business mix, being a much more hands on alternative to Management Consultancy. Providing the temporary provision of management resources and skills, Interim Management can be seen as the short term assignment to manage a period of transition, crisis or change within an organisation. In this situation, a permanent candidate may be unnecessary or impossible to find at short notice as there may be a skills or availability shortage within the organisation.

It is estimated that the Interim Management industry is worth approximately a billion pounds a year in the United Kingdom – that is big business by anyone's standards. Across all sectors, tens of thousands of interims are employed to cover unexpected gaps, deliver key projects, or drive change and growth. Interims are seen as a source of competitive advantage which is the best description of the way they are used in today's market.

Sought after interims are:

- Experienced independent executives or project managers
- Experts in their field with specialist skills
- High level performers with gravitas and a proven track record of delivery and achievement
- Engaged by businesses on a project basis to solve problems
- Required to hit the ground running and deliver results quickly before moving on to the next assignment
- Perceptive, tenacious, flexible and adaptable to new environments
- Strong communicators with excellent interpersonal and people management skills
- Able to see the bigger picture while maintaining a hands on operational focus
- Able to readily engage stakeholders
- Able to operate autonomously or as a part of a team as required
- Looking for Interim Management as a career choice rather than a stepping stone to the next permanent job

Common characteristics of interims

Across all sectors and nearly all functions, successful interims tend to demonstrate one characteristic in common: they are able to swiftly engage diverse groups of stakeholders. That ability is so important in an interim assignment, since interims need to hit the ground running, very often executing projects or implementing initiatives that span a number of organisational departments, as well as internal and external stakeholders at all levels.

Interim assignments at the senior level also require the capability to coach and mentor, since they are there to leave a legacy of value by transferring knowledge, rather than creating a culture of dependency (which has earned management consultancy a bad name in recent times). Even without the reforms and financial challenges, many organisations value the "task and finish" approach that interim managers bring to a project. The interim manager's career depends on each assignment resulting in an excellent outcome. It is also true that interim managers can be objective and speak hard truths, often helping new solutions to emerge, without worrying about their job prospects within the organisation.

Interim Management is difficult to get into but once you develop a reputation you can be in constant demand and make a great living. Interim Management might also be an option to sit within a portfolio career. Does this sound like you? If so Interim Management could be an option.

What is the difference between an interim and a temp or contractor?

An important distinction to make is the difference between the temp/contract market and genuine interim roles. While temporary roles are typically tactical (maintaining steady state), interim roles require genuine change agents who can demonstrate knowledge transfer, legacy creation, and a consistently compelling return on investment.

Some people look at the interim route for the lifestyle benefits of not having a permanent role. However, the reality can be very different. At senior level, interims tend to agree that they are pursuing a vocational call; the challenge of short term, high pressure assignments that place responsibility and accountability squarely on their shoulders. For many, the challenge and excitement of moving between organisations, even sectors or countries is far more of a draw than any perceived flexibility.

Coaching And Mentoring

Both coaching and mentoring are processes that enable both individual and business clients to achieve their full potential. Although similar, there are fundamental differences and views vary widely as to their exact nature. The following definitions have served me as the basis for training many managers over the years to embrace coaching and mentoring.

(i) Mentoring

What is mentoring?

- Derived from Greek mythology - Odysseus, King of Ithaca, went to fight the Trojan War and entrusted his son Telemachus to the care and direction of his entrusted friend, Mentor
- 'Mentor' is now synonymous with trusted adviser, friend, teacher, wise person
- Oxford dictionary definition 'experienced and trusted adviser'

How does mentoring work?

Mentoring enables an individual (mentee) to work with and follow in the path of an 'older and wiser' colleague who is the Confidante, Teacher, Role Model, Adviser, Friend, Helper who can pass on knowledge, experience and open doors to otherwise out of reach opportunities. I was Mentor to a number of people in my management career and you may also have mentored various subordinates to help them develop their careers. Or you may have developed an area of specialism which you could demonstrate as an expert and mentor newcomers.

External mentors are only different in the fact that they are independent of the organisation, therefore have no line responsibility for the 'mentee'. External mentors are being heavily used in a number of different ways to support businesses e.g.:

- Business start-up
- Business growth
- Young entrepreneurs
- Specific individual progression within organisations (especially senior executives) where they do not have the internal resource

There are a number of charities and social enterprises which have funding for mentoring schemes to support a range of people. They are constantly looking for skilled professionals to train with them, often to achieve accreditations. Such roles are usually, but not always, voluntary rather than self employed fee paying roles. However, as with other work experience, they can be an excellent way for you to gain credibility as an external mentor to ultimately benefit you in the longer term.

(ii) Coaching

What is Coaching?

Coaching gained massively in popularity in the nineties and into the new millennium, as individuals and businesses started to realise the transformational value that the coaching approach can bring. This is especially true at key times of change to enable people or businesses to move from where they are now to where they want to be. This is what excites me about coaching. There are a million and one definitions of coaching, here is mine: *"Coaching is facilitating the process of unlocking potential to achieve specific personal or business goals."* There are many more complex definitions. However, this works for me as it is simple and I hope you agree, self explanatory.

Essentially, Coaching is a form of personal development. It is the process by which individuals are enabled, through questioning and discussion to achieve specific goals e.g. to change careers, to solve problems. Or they may wish to transfer their learning to the workplace, in order to improve their personal performance, gain insights about themselves, their capabilities and potential.

How does coaching work?

- Developing an individual's performance by unlocking their capabilities through guided questioning, the use of coaching tools and conversation
- Supporting the coachee as a facilitator, helping to raise their awareness through analysis and reflection
- Facilitating the coachee to arrive at their own ideas and solutions

- A good coach should be able to develop a powerful relationship with the coachee based on honest and nonjudgmental dialogue
- Challenging perceptions and behaviour in a way that will enable the coachee to make significant transformations or performance improvements
- Because coaching involves the participation of the coachee to find their own solutions and agree the actions they will take, it drives deeper and more lasting behavioural change than other forms of training

In general, although there will be exceptions, coaching should not be directional, as the coach does not provide answers to specific problems. Instead they will facilitate the process of self resolution through specific questioning. Therefore the coach does not need to be an expert in the specific area requiring development but highly skilled in questioning and active listening. However, there inevitably comes a point in the coaching relationship when the coachee will ask the coach for very specific advice or recommendations. When thinking about developing a coaching practice, it pays you to become an expert in a specific niche so you can add even more credibility and value to the coaching relationship.

There are numerous forms of speciality or niche coaching. To help me get my book project off the ground, I worked with Leda Sammarco, a 'writer's coach'. Leda was recommended to me as someone who could help me put structure around my book idea and turn it into reality.

I owe Leda a huge debt, as although I have written dozens of articles, writing a book is a whole different ball game. I would not have engaged Leda if I did not know she was a specialist in her field, as boy did I have some questions for her!

Sports coaching tends to be much more directional, although a good coach will often question the coachee about why something is either working well or not, before giving their view. This is a much more powerful approach, as the coachee will often give reasons and thoughts that the coach may not have considered. The coach might only be looking at things from a technical perspective, rather than physical or psychological.

Other forms of coaching to be aware of:

- Life Coaching
- Executive Coaching
- Corporate/Business Coaching
- Small Business Coaching
- Group/Team Coaching
- Relationship Coaching
- Parent Coaching
- Retirement Coaching
- Youth Coaching

In my niche as a Career Coach, I specialise in redundancy support (outplacement) and career change mainly for professionals and executives. Although I work with all levels of people, I made the decision to focus on these aspects and client groups as I enjoy them the most. It also makes it easier for me to market my services rather than trying to be all things to all people.

Other forms of coaching will also have their 'micro niches' e.g. Relationship Coaching. I know a number of coaches who specialise in Divorce Coaching. This is a sad statement in itself but clearly there is a need and they are making a good living in this particular niche. I mentioned my associate Debbie Smith, a Personal Branding and Impact Coach, in Chapter three. Although Debbie works with many clients, she has targeted female executives and professionals. The reasons: firstly because of her affinity with this group but also because there is a real need. There is a widely held view that female professionals struggle with issues around confidence, self belief and image. As a result they can often fail to create the impact required to compete with male counterparts, losing out on key jobs or not achieving their true financial worth. Coaching is a great way to overcome this.

If you wish to become a coach, I suggest you develop a niche that taps into your personal values, needs, interests and passions. You can then build your knowledge base and learn any new skills required, although your true niche may take time to evolve. It will also pay you to gain a professional coaching qualification, as it is becoming increasingly difficult to get work without one. Coaching has become a very crowded and competitive market. By finding your right niche and having the right qualifications you will have a much greater chance of success.

Associate Work

Instead of being totally reliant on marketing yourself or your business, another option is for you to work for an established business, which uses a team of associates in your field of specialism e.g. Training. This is exactly what my company does. As my company has grown over the years, I have continually added to my associate team for specialist projects e.g. Outplacement, Executive, Management and Team Development.

When I started out as self employed, in addition to marketing and delivering projects for my own business,

I was an associate for a training company and have also been an associate for various HR and Outplacement Consultancies. The benefits are that you do not have to look for the business but the downside is that you are unlikely to be able to negotiate your fees, as these will be set by the company. Being an associate is also a good option as part of a portfolio career.

Health Warning...

As an associate, you will need to work under the guidelines of the company engaging you. This usually means working under their brand rather than yours. Some companies insist you sign an associate agreement before you undertake any work. If so, be especially mindful of any clauses which may affect the ownership and use of your own intellectual property.

Virtual Assistants

If you have previously held a highly responsible secretarial, PA or administrative role, have excellent PC and organisational skills and are looking for the flexibility to work from home around your family commitments, this could be an ideal option for you. A virtual assistant (typically abbreviated to VA) is typically self employed (although some might be employed by a large VA company) and provides remote professional administrative, technical, creative or social media assistance to small businesses on an hourly, project specific or ongoing basis. With modern technology it is possible for a skilled VA to perform a range of key tasks, adding real value to a number of different small businesses, rather than just working for one company. I know many VA's who have interesting portfolio careers with their VA work being the main income strand combined with other home based activities to achieve their income and lifestyle requirements.

With new communication tools and transmission technologies, it is now possible to have a Virtual Assistant who can answer your phone remotely without the caller's knowledge. This is an excellent way for small businesses to add a personal touch in the form of a receptionist without the additional cost of hiring someone, whilst also providing 24/7 coverage.

I engaged the services of a recommended VA to transcribe my first two audio books. This proved invaluable and a huge time saver. Also, rather unexpectedly, they recommended my products to others, which was an added bonus. I would definitely use them again for other specialist admin support on a project basis, as they are experts in such work and I am not!

E-Lancing

This is a massively growing trend for freelancers to undertake work, usually remotely, which is commissioned by employers through e-lancing websites e.g. Elance.com and Freelancer.com. These sites provide a huge portal for businesses to post projects online for freelancers to then battle it out pitching their skills and rates to win the work. It is rapidly becoming an option for newly redundant workers looking at novel ways to generate an ad hoc income, often as part of a portfolio career and lifestyle approach. It's also great for companies looking for low cost alternatives to fixed staff overheads. In demand professionals range from app developers, graphic designers, web developers to translators and voice over artists.

Health Warning...

Although e-lancing does offer another useful option to generate income, your competition will be global, including many skilled counterparts in third world and upcoming economies, who are fast becoming masters of marketing themselves at ultra competitive rates. As with any business opportunity, you must do your homework first and research thoroughly to determine if this cut throat marketplace is right for you. You don't want to spend precious time pitching for work at rates you cannot afford, as this will be counterproductive, won't it?

Web Based Businesses

The internet has created a whole new generation of millionaires, and quite a few billionaires, since its inception. Globalisation suddenly had a whole new vehicle to make it real and entrepreneurs had a completely new route to market. What are now iconic global brands such as Amazon, eBay and Google sprang up from nowhere in no time at all. However, the internet has also enabled any entrepreneur with a website to trade online and build a business from a home PC, laptop, iPad or similar device.

Starting an online business can be as simple as setting up a basic shop on eBay to sell a few wholesale items, to coming up with a completely new online concept with a novel way of monetising it. The beauty of the online business is that it can work for just about anyone. You don't need a fancy degree or to be based in any particular location to succeed. You can also start off small, work on your business part time or even view it as a hobby before you decide whether to commit to it. You could turn a hobby into a business or sell products by mail order or provide a service directly to customers online. The key criteria:

- You are opportunistic
- Reasonably IT savvy or if not, you have somebody specialist working on your behalf
- You have good business acumen

Looking at these criteria, maybe running a web based business now sounds appealing and something you could seriously consider?

Forex Trading (Foreign Exchange)

Although forex is the largest financial market in the world, it is relatively unfamiliar territory for small traders. Forex was primarily the domain of large financial institutions, multinational corporations and secretive hedge funds. How times have changed with the explosion of the internet. With minimal training you can quickly start trading as an individual investor. The majority of people I know who do trade, have made it part of a portfolio career to supplement income from other sources. And of course, there are some people for whom it is their primary source of income.

What is the Forex Market used for?

The Forex market is a global decentralized financial market for the exchange of currencies. Forex trading involves transactions in which one party purchases a quantity of one currency by paying in a quantity of another currency. Around the world various financial centres act as hubs for trading between a wide range of different types of buyers and sellers, 24 hours a day except weekends. It is the foreign exchange market that determines the value of one country's currency relative to another's e.g. UK pound vs. the US dollar. The Forex market also provides a medium for speculation which works to add deeper liquidity into the market, making exchange rates less volatile. The "carry-trade" is facilitated via the Forex market. This is a trade in which investors can buy high yielding currencies against low yielding currencies and profit from the higher yielding interest rate.

Health Warning...

I know people who 'play' the Forex market. Although you can stand to make substantial gains, similar to stocks and shares, you are in effect 'gambling' on the currency market, so you clearly need to be aware of the risks as well as the upside.

Product Creation – Developing Information Products

Have you ever thought it would be great to earn income from a passion, interest or knowledge you have by sharing it with others, regardless of whether you're physically working? How cool would it be to earn income while you are sleeping, on holiday enjoying yourself or when you aren't well enough to work, whilst also making a difference to the lives of other people? There are a number of ways to generate passive income i.e. rather than swapping time for money, you earn income from information products you have created using your expertise e.g.:

- Audio books
- Downloadable MP3s or other high perceived value digitally downloadable products

- Paid for prerecorded webinars and teleseminars
- Online and home study programmes
- Books and E books
- DVD or CD recordings from seminars and workshops
- Monthly subscriptions to membership sites

In today's world of instant access to information and knowledge, being able to create high quality products, at surprisingly low cost, can open up a whole new world of lucrative income opportunities.

What do you need to produce information products?

- A website set up to sell online products with an integrated shopping cart
- A passion, interest, or other knowledge and expertise to share with others
- Technology to produce and edit your product e.g. webinar or audio book
- A strong social media presence e.g. Facebook, Twitter and LinkedIn
- Marketing support or understanding of how to get your product to market

I still marvel and get the same thrill today when I receive emails on holiday telling me someone has just purchased one of my audio books or online programmes, while I am enjoying myself! Like most modern technology, this is becoming cheaper to buy and easier to use by the day. You can find someone you know, or through your networks, to outsource the technical stuff, as I do and you only focus on being the information resource. Whatever approach you take, you put in the hard work up front to develop your product and can then reap the rewards afterwards, time and again! So, what knowledge and expertise do you have that you could turn into information products? Lots I'm sure.

Affiliate Schemes

Simply put, affiliate programmes, also called **associate programmes**, are arrangements in which an online merchant website pays affiliate websites a commission to send them traffic or sell their products. These affiliate websites post links to the merchant site and are paid according to a particular agreement. This agreement is usually based on the number of people the affiliate sends to the merchant's site, or the number of people they send who buy something or perform some other action. Some arrangements pay according to the number of people who visit the page containing their merchant site's banner advertisement.

Basically, if a link on an affiliate site brings the merchant site traffic or money, the merchant site pays the affiliate site according to their agreement. Recruiting affiliates is an excellent way to sell products online, but it can also be a cheap and effective marketing strategy; it's a good way to get the word out about your site.

There are at least three parties in an affiliate programme transaction:

- The customer
- The affiliate site
- The merchant site

In 1996, Jeff Bezos, CEO and founder of Amazon.com, popularized this idea as an Internet marketing strategy.

Amazon.com attracts affiliates to post links to individual books for sale on Amazon.com, or for Amazon.com in general, by promising them a percentage of the profits if someone clicks on the link and then purchases books or other items. The affiliate helps make the sale, but Amazon.com does everything else. They take the order, collect the money and ship the book to the customer. With over 500,000 affiliate Web sites now participating, Amazon.com's programme is a resounding success.

Over the past few years, affiliate programmes have grown enormously in popularity, taking many interesting forms. For many websites that don't deal much in e-commerce (selling products or services online) themselves, functioning as an affiliate is a good way to participate in e-commerce. This could be another simple way for you to earn passive income i.e. not swapping time for money but by riding on the back of other companies' need to sell products by expanding their distribution networks. Equally, for someone like me, who has a range of online products, this is a way for me to get much wider exposure by finding affiliates to market my products.

Multi Level Marketing

Multi Level Marketing, or MLM, is a system for selling goods or services through a network of distributors. Multi level marketing, also called network marketing, is a flexible way to create a second part time income stream that has the potential to develop into a full time business occupation. People who join multi level marketing sales operations do so self employed and therefore are responsible for managing their own tax matters. After paying a joining fee and completing the training period, new members become known as independent distributors. Remuneration is directly related to their sales performance and the performance of people who join their sales team. The whole concept of multilevel marketing depends upon word of mouth with distributors selling to individuals who subsequently join the sales effort by becoming members of the team.

MLM – A marketing system that's stood the test of time

The most successful MLM companies have been established for a number of years and have developed their product range, business organisation and training programmes to maximise returns. Tupperware have been holding their famous parties for over 60 years. Avon cosmetics have been established over 50 years; Herbalife and Forever Living have been trading for over 30 years. Utility Warehouse, the top rated Which Report utility provider, is another increasingly popular example of a well respected MLM organisation.

Joining a MLM has a low cost of entry, especially as they usually provide all the training and support you will need to get started and become successful. You are "signing up" to represent that company's product and services and business opportunities. You can share the rewards from this system of business operation if you're willing to put in the hard work at the beginning. Once you've created a critical mass of sales, fed by a combination of your own personal sales and income generated by your down line team, then you should expect to see your total income really take off. MLM has made many millionaires but it is not for everyone. The work you have done in Step 2 around your Values and Needs plus Step 3 around your *true marketability* will help you determine whether MLM is something you may wish to pursue.

Franchises

Buying a franchise gives your commercial plans a head start by adopting an already successful business model. There's a lot to be said for opting for the franchise route, but as with everything you need to thoroughly research any opportunity, because a franchisor is the business rights owner of the operation concept. A franchisee is someone who buys the licence rights from the franchisor to operate the business in a particular location for an agreed period of time. A financial investment gives you a readymade business package.

Business format franchising – where full training is provided, together with use of trademarks and a complete system of doing business to include hiring and training staff, site selection, shop fitting and design plus advertising and marketing support. McDonald's, Burger King, Subway and Domino's Pizza are examples of business format franchising. Be aware that a substantial financial investment is required to take on a major high street name like McDonald's and Burger King. To open a McDonald's restaurant can cost anything from £125,000. A franchisee will also be expected to have a healthy financial reserve for working capital.

Products and trade name franchising – the key contribution here is the product or service to be sold. The franchisee takes on the identity and branding and acts as an official representative of the parent company. Trademarks and logos are provided, as well as advertising, sales and marketing support. The business investor buys the products from the brand name company under the franchise law and sells them to interested parties. This type of operation is well established in the automotive and soft drinks markets.

There are multitudes of franchise opportunities available in almost every business discipline, including accountancy firms, office cleaning companies, HR consultancies, travel agencies etc. If franchising appeals, explore franchise opportunities that:

- Appeal to you and to your personality
- Are in high demand
- Have little or no direct competition in your local area
- Nationally, or even internationally known brand with proven consumer / trade demand
- Clear and unambiguous licence terms to define franchise territory and agreement period
- Access to signage (if relevant) plus sales and marketing support
- Full initial training – for brand, product and business operation
- Access to ongoing training – and any free, or payment terms of, future training
- Back office business support systems
- Details of the financial status and track record of franchisor
- Provide evidence of a profitable business model

The principle is simple - some companies choose to grow, not by developing in the conventional way but, by granting a licence to others to sell their product or service. There are clear advantages to this.

As the voice and self regulating body of the franchising industry in the UK, the British Franchise Association (bfa), is well placed to educate individuals and businesses about the opportunities that franchising, as a successful business model, can bring. The bfa offers a number of franchise seminars at a range of locations across the UK.

Buying Into An Existing Business In Part Or Whole

If you have received a good redundancy package or you are in the fortunate position of being in a strong financial situation, you may wish to consider buying a business outright or buying into a business. *Here are two approaches to consider:*

- Become involved with your chosen going concern as a part time employee – paid or unpaid
- Buying an existing business outright and taking total management control

The nature and level of involvement could depend on your skills, experience and degree of financial contribution. This is a stepping stone approach before purchase and you'll get to know the business intimately before you commit, and you will discover the strengths and weaknesses before you invest. Working within the company before you decide on any further financial commitment will provide on the job experience. What appears to be a healthy profitable organisation on the outside may reveal a different, more sobering reality from the inside.

Due diligence

Before you take any major decisions or make any investment into an ongoing concern, it is important to conduct various aspects of due diligence to establish a number of criteria:

- Who the legal owners are and the shareholding breakdown of the business.
- Looking back over company balance sheets and trading records.
- Checking the current performance - sales, profits, cash flow, outstanding debts, current bank balance etc.

Always seek professional advice from a trusted and recommended source before you enter into any agreement.

The information in this section of the Chapter is purely to act as an aide memoire and highlight a selection of options that might be possible for you to consider, although there are many more. You will need to do in depth research on any aspects you are particularly interested in. Some will be right for you and some definitely not. This is all about CHOICE!

Self Employment – Starting Your Own Business

Self employment is an attractive alternative as a change of direction, following redundancy. In my experience, it can prove to be even more so if you have previously harboured thoughts of being your own boss, although many people decide to take the leap of faith who have never given self employment any thought whatsoever. Successful self employment requires a similar mindset to winning through redundancy. However, the same rule of thumb applies i.e. 'one size does not fit all'. Self employment potentially allows you the flexibility to choose your own hours and to work from home, around family commitments. Of course, it is not always like this, especially when you start out. At the time of writing, almost 4.2 million people were registered as self employed in the UK. This is the highest figure since records began in 1992, according to the Office for National Statistics (ONS). If you are serious about joining them, you will firstly need to research all of the following and maybe more, depending on what your business does:

- Your business idea
- Your business name
- Your competition
- The most suitable trading structure e.g. Sole Trader, Partnership or Limited Company
- Business start-up funding / financing your business
- Marketing / business development
- Pricing
- Registering for taxes and National Insurance
- Business premises i.e. home based, offices etc
- Your training needs
- Technology requirements
- Developing a business plan

The good news is there is a wealth of information available via the internet from sites such as http://www.startups.co.uk, through various local and regional government agencies, from many of the major high street banks and various regional and national start-up exhibitions. If you decide to set up your own limited company, this is no longer a huge ordeal as you can do so online in a few minutes from around only twenty pounds! Basically you can no longer use 'red tape' as an excuse not to set up. So what is stopping you then? Maybe you?

Every Situation Is Different

Whether self employment is right for you will depend on what you're looking to achieve and this is where re-evaluation and exploring opportunities are so important. If you decide you want to change career and set up a business of your own, there are many implications to consider. Setting up as self employed is very simple, but how straightforward your business start-up will be depends totally on the type of business you are planning. An unusual example was a client who decided to set up a very niche style of coffee shop. This is clearly not your every day type of business, so it needed a huge amount of research, especially around finding the right type of property in the right location, financing, looking at the whole end to end process, return on investment etc. It was clear this would take many months of planning, so we needed a contingency. He decided his short term goal was to do other self employed work, utilising some of the skills we established from his true marketability, from which he could generate income quickly. This included language tuition and swimming instruction plus some other interests he quickly turned into income streams, while he was developing his 'dream' business. So let's now look at what self employment or starting a business can offer you, warts and all, as it is not right for everyone.

Weighing Up The Pros And Cons

Let's now consider whether the self employment pros outweigh the self employment cons. Not everyone has the same good experience of working from home, working alone, managing staff or running a business, so self employment or being your own boss isn't suited to everyone. You must weigh up the options to discover your own pros and cons so you can make an informed decision: is self employment or starting a business right for you?

To help your decision making process, the list below is a typical example of some key pros and cons of self employment. There are no right or wrong answers as you may have completely different views depending on your attitude to these statements.

Example table

SELF EMPLOYMENT	
PROs	CONs
Be your own boss	You will have to make provision for your own pension and no employer benefits
Reap the rewards of your success	If you are unwell and unable to work you will not earn anything
You do not have to pay income tax until the January following the end of your first year of trading	You will not get paid if you take a holiday
National insurance costs less	You will probably have to work long hours
You can claim tax relief on many items	You will be responsible for any losses
You will have greater freedom than if you were employed	Possible isolation and loneliness (note: collaborations and support networks help overcome this)

No daily commute if you work from home or have premises close to where you live	Constantly marketing and looking for work
Choice – where you work, the work you do, who you work with, how you work, when you work, how you dress	Peaks and troughs of work and income
Working around family commitments	Lack of employer security

If you are excited by the pros of self employment you have highlighted from this exercise, look at ways in which you can overcome the cons either now or in the medium to long term future. Or do the pros outweigh enough of the cons to make this a viable option for you? Equally do you agree with the pros and cons? If not make up your own list to work through and decide. There is no right or wrong answer but only what feels right for you.

Health Warning...

Before you commit to self employment, if you have a spouse or partner, **it is essential to get them on board first.** This applies, not just if you set up a company and may need substantial funding, but as a matter of course. *Why?* Because you are unlikely to be able to guarantee regular income for some while and every business has peaks and troughs, so your income is rarely steady. This is a total change from having a regular salary each month, requires a very different mindset and careful household financial management.

During troughs, you need to have enough income coming in from your partner (if he or she is working). If your partner isn't working, you must ensure you have enough cash reserves behind you to keep both your business and household going. There are also the physical demands of developing, growing and managing your business. When the peaks come, you have to take full advantage, so it will be all hands to the pump and could mean you working excessively long hours and even 7/7. Likewise when you are working on key developmental activity, this can be equally demanding on your time and energy, so your partner must be totally supportive. I shared this same thinking with an ex next door neighbour, who had decided to set up his own building business. He had a wife and young family and I feared his wife had not bought into the concept. He was constantly working six or seven days a week and never got round to doing the work that was desperately needed to modernise their own house, which she resented. It drove a wedge between them and their marriage ended in disaster. Be warned as you don't want the same to happen to you, do you?

Businesses Evolve

There is a strongly held view by business gurus that businesses need to constantly reinvent themselves to compete with the changing landscape, demands of new technology and so on. Just as you need to do yourself following redundancy. Therefore if you decide to set up a business don't feel that it will always have to stay the same. The majority of businesses evolve and change over time. Look at Sir Richard Branson. He has spent his career building up businesses, like Virgin Records, selling them then moving into new areas e.g. Airline, Mobile phones and Finance. My business bears no relationship today to what it was when I started ten years ago. Most businesses will evolve and you will naturally gravitate to the work you enjoy the most, your passions and interests. Although I had decided I did not want a full time Reward and Benefits job again, I was good at this type of work. When I set up my business, word got around and I was suddenly in demand for Reward and Benefits consultancy, which helped to get my business off to a good start. However, I wasn't passionate enough about this work and although I could command excellent consultancy rates, I was keen to develop my real passions, especially around Career and People Development. As a result, I made sure my Reward and Benefits work became only a part of my portfolio career and not my mainstream business and phased it out altogether after a couple of years.

Over the years, I have continued to refine our business services and products to specialise in aspects of business I enjoy most. Therefore in addition to Career Development, we have kept focus on Executive, Management and Team Development, which all require associate support on projects as and when needed. To this day my business is still evolving, especially by creating new career development products to sell online, speaking and of course writing. My wife is now a co-director and delivers career and education coaching, working with young people. The key is to keep control of your business focus in line with your passions and key areas of interest, so any changes reflect this - 'passions build £'s'!

Health Warning...

Do not, under any circumstances, set up a business exclusively doing something you are good at but don't really enjoy, just because you need to generate income quickly. Although it might work initially it cannot be sustained. This is the same principle as having an employed job you don't enjoy. You won't be fulfilled and people buy people, so your lack of passion will come across to everybody you come into contact with, which is a recipe for disaster.

Mind mapping your decision

If you are someone who likes to use mind maps to brainstorm and collect your thoughts, it can be an excellent way to help you work through your options to decide what job, career or work to do. If you are a very visual person, you might find that mind mapping your options improves the way that you record information, and supports and enhances creative problem solving to aid your decision making process. Within your mind map you can build in options for employment, self employment or a portfolio career and lifestyle. There are many excellent online mind mapping tools available these days. Some offer 'bells and whistles' but if you want something simple, there are usually free versions which are fine to start you off.

✎ *Exercise – Taking the Leap of Faith*

Now you have had the opportunity to consider some alternative options, to help 'untangle some weeds in your mind', let's now take a look at the Leap of Faith exercise, which will challenge you even further. Carefully think through your answers to these key questions. They will provide you with more clarity and help you make informed decisions to take you to the final Step of the Cycle with greater confidence.

Q1. What would you do if you were not afraid?

Consider your possibilities, what fears you have around these and aim to banish them!

Q2. What would you do if money were no object or all jobs paid the same?

Q3. What problems can you solve that other people will pay for?

Consider your range of skills and talents and how you can use these to earn income

Q4. What is stopping you/holding you back?

Consider the barriers/obstacles to achieving your dream and what can you reframe to help you take the leap of faith into new work you love?

Q5. What have you learned from this exercise?

What positive action can you take right now?

How did I take my leap of faith?

This was yet another example of how other people can see things in you that you cannot see for yourself. Having decided I'd had enough of working for other people and wanted to be my own boss, I networked and reconnected with as many people as I possibly could, who I knew had become self employed and set up their own business. I asked them what they had learnt, what they would do differently if they started again and also what they thought I could do in my business and would be good at. I had a few ideas of problems I could solve that people would pay for but nothing concrete.

Everybody was telling me that I had a natural talent for developing people and helping them to achieve their potential. The evidence was staring me in the face but I couldn't see it! Now I had untangled the weeds in my mind, it was much easier to focus on my business offering and the feedback enabled me to develop my business strap line '*helping you unlock your potential*'. However, it was still scary but as I have stated, you must turn your fear into focus. So, I finally decided to go for it.

Having set my intent, things started happening, as I explained in the Introduction. My next leap of faith, was winning my first fee paying work. I remember driving to a meeting with a contact, for some potential Reward and Benefits consultancy, feeling a mixture of excitement, fear and trepidation! I had been out of work for almost a year, had never done any consultancy work in my life and how on earth was I going to prove I had the knowledge and expertise they required? Maybe you also recognise these limiting beliefs? Fear not!

Was what happened remarkable or more likely, just proof, we are our own worst enemies? In the meeting I went into autopilot immediately, asking key questions, challenging, really getting to grips with the issues the company was facing and making positive suggestions to take the project forward. Suddenly I was being told, I had exactly the right attitude and approach, so when was I going to start? My emotions driving home were a mixture of euphoria, disbelief, relief and wondering what all the fuss was about! The reality was I had demonstrated my knowledge and expertise, skills and attributes in exactly the same way I would have done in my previous employed role, which resulted in winning this project, then many others.

So, why do people make such a song and dance about taking the leap of faith into self employment? I'm sure you have already worked this out, haven't you? Self employment or running your own business is similar to winning through redundancy, as your mindset is key! You are still the same person but you are now working for yourself as opposed to an employer, without your colleagues and other support services you may have relied on. This is just another reframe, as you learnt in Chapter one. So, what reason are you giving yourself for not using your true marketability in a self employed role to successfully start up a business of your own? Your answer will determine whether you are now ready to take your '*leap of faith*'!

Summary

Step 5 - key learning points:

- You do have the CHOICE to reinvent yourself to become the architect of your own future and decide what work you want to do!
- If you are still unclear, imagine you are untangling the weeds in your mind to achieve the CLARITY you want
- Six months is a psychological barrier to overcome but only if you make it one
- When you are ready, get serious about your 'campaign' as time will fly past
- Use the power of The Universal Laws - *'success goes where your energy flows'*
- By changing your mindset around the need to have a JOB, you have multiple choices to decide on the type of work you do next
- Mind mapping your options can help your decision making process

- Understand the pros and cons of self employment before you jump in headfirst
- Getting additional support from a coach or mentor could make all the difference
- Your mindset and belief will help you make the transition into self employment

Congratulations, you are now ready to move to the final step of the Career Navigation Cycle - **Taking Positive Action!**

CHAPTER 6

Taking Positive Action – Step 6

"The same wind blows on us all. It is not the blowing of the wind that determines your destination but the setting of a better sail"

Jim Rohn, Entrepreneur, Author & Motivational Speaker, 1930-2009

Congratulations you have reached the final step of the Cycle and are now well on the way to completing your voyage of self discovery to achieve a successful outcome. This is where the dawn of reality will definitely kick in, if it hasn't before, as your future can seem exciting or scary or both! The sixth and final step of the process can see you retreat back into your comfort zone, unless you have the right motivation, support and courage. It is about trusting that you have done enough preparation; now you simply need to take a leap of faith to achieve your breakthrough career transition or change.

Just do it

This Chapter could be summed up by a simple matter of the three words made world famous by Nike *"Just Do it!"* Fortunately, I will give you much more practical help than this, to ensure you do have the tools to help you through this final step of the process. However, the Nike slogan is absolutely spot on, as it is **only you** who can ultimately take responsibility to successfully *navigate your way to a brighter future.*

If not now, when will you do what you love?

If you don't follow through on this key final step of the Cycle and transition into doing a job, career or work you love, then when will you? You don't want to be like many people who always talk about doing work they love but are never bold enough to take the action required, do you? I'm sure you don't want to spend the rest of your life thinking 'what if?'

In my case, my motivation for taking positive action to set up my business was driven by a strong determination to sign off from the Job Centre. When I finished my government funded support programme, I made a personal commitment to never sign on again! This was coupled with an enlightening conversation I had with my dear mum a while before, when she asked me what I was going to do next. I told her I was going to set up a business of my own, to which her response (bearing in mind she has no interest in business or finance) was *"I'm not surprised. Anyway, what have you got to lose and what is the worst that can happen?"* Put this way, when I wasn't earning anything at all at the time, the answer was simple *"Nothing, I'm not afraid to work hard for something I believe in, and if it doesn't work out I can look at getting another job"*, which I had no intention of doing. These were the only incentives I needed to take positive action and I have never looked back.

Twelve years on I continue to re-evaluate and look at new ways to stretch myself and realise my long term passions and unfulfilled potential, especially my writing. Through writing blogs, articles for trade journals and various personal development websites in the UK and US, this has evolved into writing this book and becoming a published author.

Looking back, my love of writing started at school editing the school magazine, writing numerous articles and my first ever career thoughts were of becoming a journalist. I believe we all have latent potential hiding inside us bursting to get out. As already highlighted, if the *WHY* is strong enough, the *WHAT* and *HOW* will follow. It is true that I was encouraged by family, friends, associates and inspiring people I met along the way. People like Leda, my book coach, Sue Blake, an amazing publicist, to whom this book is dedicated and most importantly, Ed Peppitt. It was Ed who came to my rescue at a turning point in the publication of the book after I had been badly let down by my initial publisher. Nonetheless, this only spurred me on and served to reiterate the value of continuing to 'take positive action' to make my dream a reality. Above all else, I had to be brave and 'take the leap of faith' to realise my dream. Therefore you, like me, can also reinvent yourself, follow your passions and make them become reality to do work you love!

Follow up and follow through – "Set a better sail"

The secret to this final stage of the Cycle is simple. You must follow up and follow through. You must have the will and desire and commitment to make your successful career transition happen and do so with positive and inspired action.

Get In Shape – Do Some Exercises

Implementing your actions will require clear plans to follow and a certain mental toughness and agility to allow you to persevere and succeed. I am therefore inviting you to enter my 'mind gym' to take some final vigorous exercise. Physical exercise promotes health and wellbeing; mental exercise will create the positive mindset to allow you to take 'positive action'.

✎ *Exercise 1 – Get Fit For Lift Off! The Five W's check*

With the focus, knowledge and wealth of new insight gained, you should have a much clearer picture of where you are, how you got there and where you are heading, helping you start the all important process of focused career planning. Imagine you are now on the launch pad ready to blast off into a new and exciting adventure of a fulfilling job, career or work. This book and your new insight is your starter 'tool kit' and you are on countdown to 'lift off'. You can be gripped by the fear of the unknown and hold back and be the 'victim' - never venturing out of your comfort zone. Or you have the opportunity to take control and be the 'architect of your own wonderful future'.

Fasten your seatbelts because the countdown has started and you are on your final checks. It is important to consider and confirm the following status in order to make a smooth take off and a successful landing into your chosen field of work and a brighter future.

WHAT - *Double check your awareness of your 'true marketability' from your life and career. Are you now clear on what you have to offer the world and have identified any learning gaps?*

WHERE - *Your interests, passions and potential fields of activity could be applied e.g. type of organisation, sector, environment, location or even starting your own business.*

WHO *- Identify your network: the people who can help (eyes, ears, and advocates); the people who can influence, coach, support and steer you in the right direction to unlock the key to your future. It is often the most unlikely people.*

WHEN *- Set a realistic timescale to achieve your successful career change with regular review points. Celebrate small wins along the way that show you are making progress.*

WHY *- Confirm your reasons, values, key motivators/ drivers and purpose for your change.*

The *Five W's* checks you have just carried out are crucial but wait; one final check has been missed otherwise you could veer off into the abyss!

HOW *- The final check needed to initiate your planning and to implement your strategy with total commitment and belief, not forgetting those all important contingencies.*

For some people, what holds them back from making a breakthrough change, aside of any fear, is often reframing a few simple aspects around their thinking about the need to have another 'job' and then taking the first steps to make change happen. The following case study will highlight an excellent example of how you can use the *Five W's* process to challenge your mindset, overcome limiting beliefs, follow your passions and achieve a successful outcome.

Linda's Story – Shifting from 'Job' mindset to a flexible working lifestyle

Following redundancy, Linda fell into the same trap I have highlighted before. Her conditioning and beliefs were based on the need for another job. However, she had a fantastic opportunity to re-evaluate and rethink what she wanted from her work and life. Having done so, it became apparent that what she was hoping to achieve would be almost impossible from a typical job, which is why she struggled for a few months. Her priorities were:

Getting some structure – Like lots of busy people, Linda found the lack of routine and structure to her days and week difficult to manage. What she wanted was something each week to look forward to. She eventually found this by contacting a friend, who ran a local charity shop, to do some voluntary work one morning a week. This was the first building block and became a key part of her life, which she now works everything else around.

Choice – After a few months out of work and turning down a couple of jobs, she realised that she wanted to focus on work she wanted to do now, following her passions, working with the people she wanted to, in locations she wanted.

Flexibility – This was one of her most important needs. The reason she turned down some jobs was because of rigid employer expectations. Linda wanted to be the architect of her own future, working on her terms.

This was clearly not a recipe for a typical job! However, once she isolated these key needs and addressed the *Five W's* questions she quickly managed to develop what has become a most interesting portfolio career and lifestyle. In her words:

"My portfolio developed quickly once I had identified what was most important to me. I made the following choices and goals:

- Give myself the flexibility to work only the days and hours I want
- Have a variety of work each week
- Take my holidays when I want to
- Source, network and identify opportunities which match my values and needs

- Continue to support and work for my local charity
- Develop my own private client base, coaching young people to realise their true potential
- Realise my dream to work with special needs children, primary, infant and nursery school children which I had long aspired to achieve but thought it too late in my career and life to make this transition
- Achieve a regular income from doing work I love, which gives me job satisfaction and above all where I feel valued"

Having set her intent, Linda achieved all these goals in a matter of months. Her working week now consists of:

1. A minimum of two days working self employed in a local school, encompassing a variety of teaching and support roles in the children's centre, primary and junior school, which changes on a flexible weekly basis
2. Up to one day a week, working voluntarily for a local charity, includes various fundraising events
3. Coaching young people on an ad hoc basis, providing pre and post education support and helping them overcome their barriers to progression
4. Last but not least, co-director of her husband's business, involved with business planning, finances, event management and general support

Linda is another excellent example of a career changer who has proved that, by following the Cycle and taking positive action, you do have CHOICE and it is never too late to do work you love!

✎ *Exercise 2 – Set Sail with the 'Four C's' Career Action Planner*

Let's now look at the *Four C's Career Action Planner:* your mission heading for the job, career or work you really want. I have used this simple but highly effective career action planner with hundreds of clients to great effect. I recommend you set this up on a spreadsheet or table, so you can keep adding new actions as you think of them. As with any action plan it is always good practice to add timescales to start and complete different tasks. Don't forget, *'what gets measured gets done!'*

<table>
<tr><td><u>Commence:</u><ul><li>Activities you should start now to take positive action and move you towards your end goal</li></ul></td><td><u>Continue:</u><ul><li>Activities which are already working for you so you can do more and build momentum</li></ul></td></tr>
<tr><td><u>Cease:</u><ul><li>Activities that are unhelpful, move you away from your goal or any negative mindset that can deter you from achieving your goal</li></ul></td><td><u>Consider:</u><ul><li>Any learning gaps and skills required to achieve your goal</li><li>The inspiration gained from reading this book, to allow you to make decisions on what to commence or cease in due course</li></ul></td></tr>
</table>

 *Exercise 3 – Relax then Stretch*

Moving from your comfort zone into your stretch zone

You don't achieve anything worthwhile in your life without moving out of your comfort zone. So let's do an exercise to help you **give yourself permission** to move out of your comfort zone and take positive action to move yourself forward into the stretch zone. Only by doing this can you take control of your life and career to become the architect of your own future.

There are two parts to this exercise. Consider the diagram below and:

(i) Make a note of the words and phrases that apply to how you have seen yourself previously

(ii) Now consider and write down the words and phrases in the Stretch Zone that relate to how you are now feeling plus those you know you need to work at in order to take positive action.

Complete the comfort zone and stretch zone exercise. Bear in mind that as you take positive action your comfort zone will shrink and your stretch zone will expand.

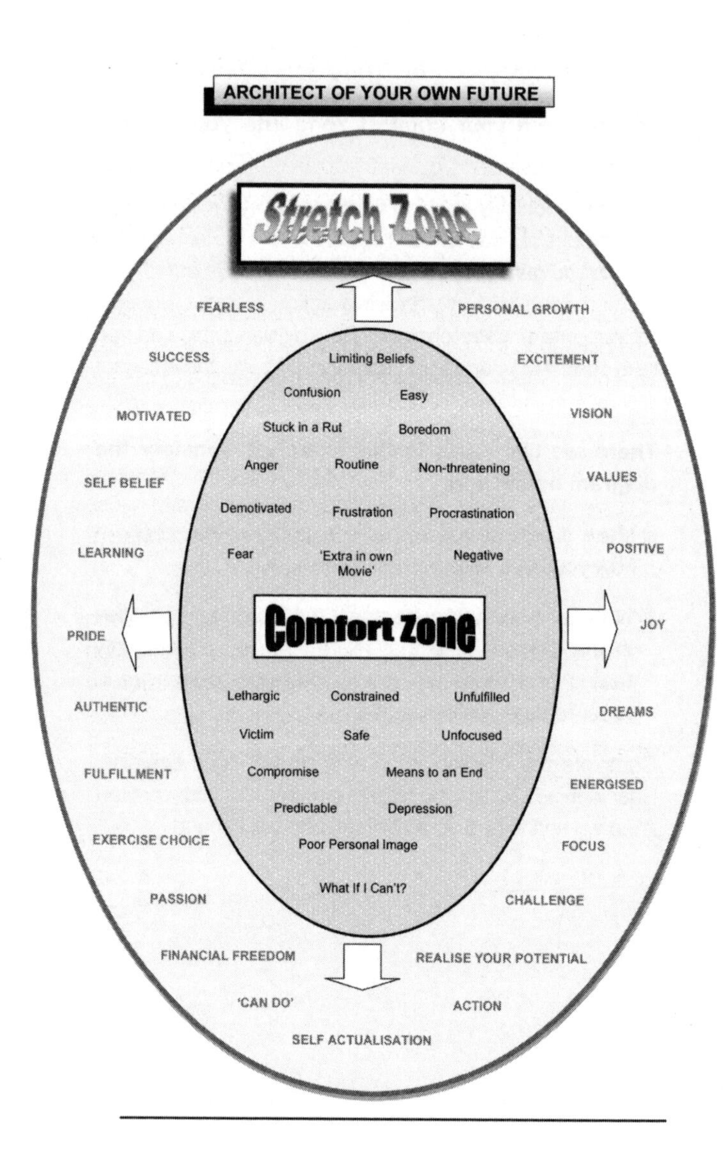

ARCHITECT OF YOUR OWN FUTURE
Stretch Zone
FEARLESS
PERSONAL GROWTH
SUCCESS
EXCITEMENT
MOTIVATED
VISION
SELF BELIEF
VALUES
LEARNING
POSITIVE
PRIDE
JOY
AUTHENTIC
DREAMS
FULFILLMENT
ENERGISED
EXERCISE CHOICE
FOCUS
PASSION
CHALLENGE
FINANCIAL FREEDOM
REALISE YOUR POTENTIAL
'CAN DO'
ACTION
SELF ACTUALISATION
Limiting Beliefs
Confusion
Easy
Stuck in a Rut
Boredom
Anger
Routine
Non-threatening
Demotivated
Frustration
Procrastination
Fear
'Extra in own Movie'
Negative
Comfort Zone
Lethargic
Constrained
Unfulfilled
Victim
Safe
Unfocused
Compromise
Means to an End
Predictable
Depression
Poor Personal Image
What If I Can't?

✎ *Exercise 4 – The Eight Key Character Traits to Achieve Successful Change*

Having focused on your action plan, let's now drill down further by looking at another important exercise to stretch you, which requires positive action by you in order to ensure your successful career transition outcome.

These eight key character traits are recognised as making the difference to achieving successful change in your life. Sooner or later you will reach this final step in the Cycle and be ready to *'take positive action'* and you will feel confident in doing so by addressing these eight traits. Some people may resist this final step, but I know that having reached this far you **will** be curious to end on a high note because you will want to achieve your successful career change or transition into a new job, career or work you love.

You have come on a long voyage of self discovery. Along the way, you will have absorbed a wealth of information and advice. This penultimate exercise is to establish how much you have grown in confidence and are ready to face the challenges ahead. Consider the eight key character traits diagram:

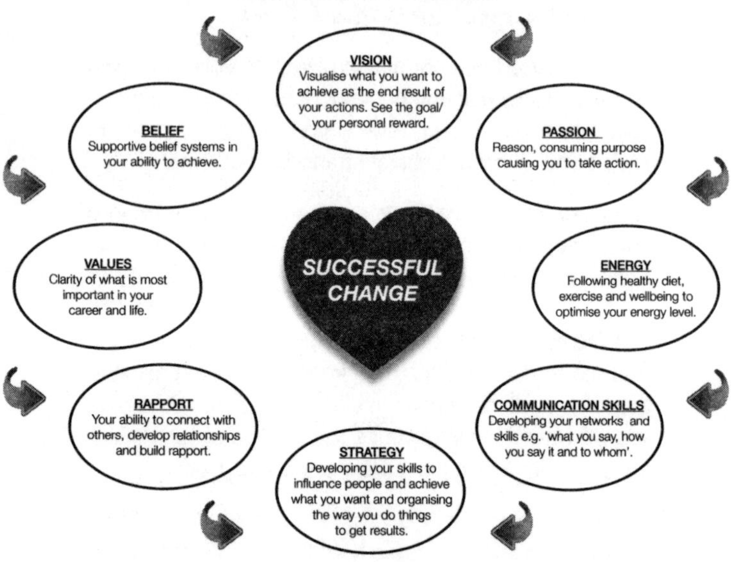

- Take each trait e.g. Passion and score yourself out of 10 on how you rate yourself now
- While you are still in transition to your next career step, it is a good strategy to do this exercise at regular intervals so you can review and measure your progress
- Each time you do this exercise, record the date by your scores to allow you to track changes over time
- When you revisit the exercise, it is important not to 'cheat' and look at your previous scores
- To get real benefit, as with all the exercises in this book, you must be totally honest with yourself
- Most importantly, by revisiting some of the exercises in this book, you can focus your energy on maximising

the traits that are already strong, whilst working even harder on those which need development to build your confidence to the level you want

- Only **you** can now take responsibility for your successful outcome!

The following case study is a wonderful example of a woman who got out of her comfort zone, really stretched herself and took positive action to turn her business idea into a reality.

Helen's story

Helen came to our Breakthrough Career Change & Transition Masterclass for two reasons:

- She had a potential redundancy opportunity with a Local Authority and wanted to work through her options to decide what to do for the best
- She was unhappy, not enjoying her job and concerned for the impact on her own life, her outlook, her family life with her husband and two young children

As a result of coming on the Masterclass, Helen realised she was in absolutely the wrong job for her. She was a square peg in a round hole and she couldn't carry on any longer! When exploring her opportunities, she decided not to wait for the redundancy opportunity. She hadn't been in the job long enough to gain any real financial benefit from a pay off and she wanted to take control of her situation and 'become the architect of her own future'. So what did Helen do? She resigned.

Was Helen bold or foolish?

To come to your conclusion, read on but also consider how Helen swiftly moved out of her comfort zone and the impact this had.

Another realisation for Helen was an appreciation of all the great skills and attributes she hadn't ever thought about, or just took for granted, as many of us do, don't we? She also had interests and passions, which she could turn into business opportunities. One of these was soft furnishings. Although, at the Masterclass, Helen was totally reluctant to move out of her comfort zone and consider running her own business, when she reflected on the day, she decided that she should not ignore all the evidence. Now was the time, now was the opportunity.

Her voyage of self discovery on the Masterclass had dramatically boosted her confidence, so she started taking note of what other people were telling her i.e. maybe she did have what was needed to set up her own business, maybe she could make it work? A few weeks after the Masterclass she took the leap of faith and set up her own soft furnishing business and enrolled on an Open University distance learning degree in soft furnishings. Helen was astounded when immediately she received interest and literally within a few months had an order book which was filled eight months in advance. Absolutely fantastic!

Helen sent me a wonderful email explaining all this and thanking me for the insight from the day which had helped transform her career and her life. Most poignantly, her final comment was that her kids said *"We've got Mum back"* and her husband said

> *"He'd got his Wife back"* and yet most importantly Helen realised that she had got her life back! These wonderful statements proved beyond doubt she had done the right thing.

So, was Helen bold or foolish?

Clearly Helen had been bold and in the process she had achieved her ideal work and life blend. She only worked four days a week, with one day to herself and had become a Mum again in the best way possible. It's a wonderful heart warming story. By investing in our Masterclass and going through the Career Navigation Cycle process on the day, Helen realised how unhappy she really was. Also, by gaining valuable insight from the group, she started to believe in herself, that she did have the skills and talents to run a successful business.

A few years on, Helen took another bold step and set up a partnership with a contact of hers and within a short space of time they were commissioned by none other than Saatchi and Saatchi. What a world of difference and just think how miserable Helen might be now if she hadn't stepped out of her comfort zone and taken some of the bold decisions she has taken over the last few years?

Learning Points

- Helen went on the same voyage of discovery you have. Like most people, the exercises proved to her she had so much more to offer than she realised, which motivated her to want to change
- Having worked her way round the Cycle and decided what to do, she then took the leap of faith with inspired and positive action to achieve her successful outcome

- If you are or were a square peg in a round hole you can take positive action to change and create the working lifestyle you want
- Remember: "anything is possible, within reason, with the right mindset, belief, skills and positive actions"
- As with all the examples in this book, Helen proved, again, that you should follow your passions and as I have said *'Success goes where your energy flows!"*

This can all be summed up beautifully by Henry David Thoreau's (Poet and Philosopher, 1817-1862) great quote:

"We must walk consciously only part way toward our goals and then leap into the dark to our success!"

✎ *Exercise 5 – Ongoing Plans and Reviews*

So, having completed the exercises so far you need now to take stock. This final exercise encourages you to reflect and review. It will also remind you that the journey never ends and that you continue to learn, grow, develop and flourish. Whichever point you have reached, you should never be complacent, so keep up the momentum and take this opportunity to consider further improvements about what you might want to do next.

How far have I come on my journey?

On the line below plot your position from 1 to 10, where 10 means getting your ideal job or work.

1 2 3 4 5 6 7 8 9 10

Next career transition steps

- How do you move on from where you are today to where you want to be?

- What is the gap made up of? e.g. If you feel you are now at 6 on the scale above, what do you see as the main barriers and key actions to make it to 10 on the scale and to achieve your ideal job, career or working lifestyle?
- Break this down into manageable chunks.

First Career Transition Steps:	Planned Completion Date:	Actual Completion Date:
1.		
2.		
3.		
I will review my progress in these first steps on:		

Outcome of first review:

- How good has my progress been? What additional coaching/support do I need?

Summary

Step 6 Key Learning Points:

- At this final step of the Cycle follow the Nike adage and "Just do it!"
- What have you got to lose by trying something different?
- Take positive action now to avoid thinking 'what if' for the rest of your life

- Work on the Five W's and Four C's to shape your direction and 'Set a better sail'
- Cease anything that is not helping you or moving you away from your end goal
- Commence any activities which you need to take positive action on NOW!
- You must move out of your comfort zone and stretch yourself to achieve success
- Build your confidence to make your change by working on the Eight Key Character Traits
- You must change your thinking and beliefs before you can do this!
- If you need structure in your working life, start by finding one thing to build from which you can look forward to each week and you will find your working week will evolve
- It is fine to do work with a mix of paid and unpaid if it works for you – you do have CHOICE!
- You can now review your progress – where you started from, what your successful career change or transition now looks like and the positive action you need to take to achieve this
- It is your future and only you can take responsibility for your successful outcome

Congratulations, you have now completed the six Steps of my Career Navigation Cycle process! I hope you have enjoyed your journey and have been inspired to take action. Please read on for some final thoughts and a fantastic case study so that you, like me and the many people you have read about, can also win through redundancy and *navigate your way to a brighter future!*

CONCLUSION

"In the end, it's not the years in your life that count; it's the life in your years!"

Abraham Lincoln
(Former US President) 1809 - 1865

This powerful quote from Abraham Lincoln is a fabulous endorsement for my own mantra, which I shared with you in Chapter two. Life is too short to be unhappy but rather than looking back on 'wasted' years you may have had, if you can change your thinking and beliefs to this perspective, take the leap of faith and full responsibility for your successful outcome, you cannot go far wrong to achieving happiness and fulfilment in your work and life.

Winning through redundancy and navigating the career transition maze is a daunting prospect for most people. However, I know that you, like me, may now realise and believe that things usually happen for a reason. Redundancy is a fantastic opportunity for you to break out of your comfort zone, take back control of your career and life to do work you really love. You may never get a better chance so take it while you can, as you don't want regrets, do you?

Become The Architect Of Your Own Future

Congratulations, you have completed what I'm sure has been an enlightening voyage of self discovery! It may have been an emotional roller coaster for you, however, you will know that I have taken great care throughout to demonstrate that my Career Navigation Cycle process works, providing that you follow each step, believe in the process and finally follow through by taking positive action. Reading this book and completing the exercises will have motivated you and have moved you closer to realise the job, career or work you aspire to and create the lifestyle you want. As a consequence, you will now be much better placed to move forward with confidence and belief of what you can do and achieve.

Toolkit For Life

Winning through redundancy and successfully relaunching your career is all about mindset. With the knowledge and insight you have gained from reading this book, you have no reason to ever be 'a square peg in a round hole' and in the wrong job. Likewise, there is no need to be like the majority of people who are unfulfilled in their job or the work they do.

You now have a redundancy support and career transition toolkit for life. Remember that this is a Cycle, so it is a process that you may go through more than once. Like riding a bike, you may need to hone your skills if you haven't used them for a while but you now have a process and developed skills you can use for the rest of your life.

In order to achieve your successful career transition, it is important to plan your onward journey and to review your progress regularly.

The Simplified Law Of Cause And Effect

The common thread that has linked every element of my Navigation Cycle has been the need to change. As your confidence has grown and mindset changed you will feel empowered to take that final *'leap of faith'* and to fly. The transformation of our thinking is wonderfully encapsulated by The Simplified Law of Cause and Effect.

When we change our	**THINKING** we change our	**BELIEFS**
When we change our	**BELIEFS** we change our	**EXPECTATIONS**
When we change our	**EXPECTATIONS** we change our	**ATTITUDES**
When we change our	**ATTITUDES** we change our	**FEELINGS**
When we change our	**FEELINGS** we change our	**BEHAVIOUR**
When we change our	**BEHAVIOUR** we change our	**RESULTS**
When we change our	**RESULTS** we change our	**LIFE**

How much have you managed to change your thinking and beliefs? If you are still stuck in your comfort zone, I suggest you reread the book or revisit the Chapter where you have got stuck, so you can move forward with renewed confidence. You may feel now is the time to engage a career coach to help 'untangle the weeds in your mind' to achieve clarity. Finally, remember career change or transition is a process, so you may move back and forth between different steps or go round the Cycle more than once, as it is a virtuous Cycle. No sooner do you get right round than you start again and have to '*let go*' of other things to then move forward and start the process again. If this is the case with you, view this as a continuation of your journey, as persistence pays and ultimately you will achieve your desired outcome.

To summarise the learning from this book, I will leave you with the inspiring story of Ruth, a most interesting client who has really embraced the Career Navigation Cycle process to follow her remarkable dream.

Ruth's Story

I met Ruth at the Forum 3 Charity exhibition a number of years ago, when I was running seminars on changing careers. Having attended my seminar and taken on board some of the learning points, Ruth acted quickly and decisively by booking on my Breakthrough Career Change and Transition Masterclass. She was still young, had a good professional job and company car. However, Ruth hated her job and wanted to take control of her career and future. Once she started working her way through the Cycle, it was small wonder she hated her job as she quickly came to realise her job was totally at odds with her values and needs and this was affecting her whole outlook on life!

Her first light bulb moment came on the Masterclass. The group work sparked her into life with new thinking. By the end of the day, she had her vision.... lions, Africa, making a difference! Another major light bulb moment was that she had never made a conscious decision about her career in her life.

She had let her friends take control of her life by influencing what she studied and where she studied for University then subsequently even her choice of job and company! Ruth now wanted to do something completely different and probably like many of you reading this book, she didn't have a clue what she wanted to do next.

The good news is that many of the exercises you have covered in Chapters one to three, really opened up her thinking and have transformed her life. Having completed her re-evaluation and understood what was important to her in her career and life and WHY, her vision of success, and worked on her survival budget, Ruth made a key commitment to reduce her mortgage to speed the process of change for her. This really was taking positive action and responsibility in a big way!

When exploring opportunities, Ruth realised she wanted to **live the dream she had never had the opportunity to do.** This set her on a whole new journey to follow her passions, interests and do what she loves with the ultimate goal to work in Africa with 'big cats'. Having completed much research, Ruth took very positive action by studying for an MSc in Wildlife Conservation, learning in her own time, around a full time job. If that's not passion and commitment I don't know what is! She also took the very important step of putting her toe in the water by volunteering at a wildlife park over weekends, a fair distance from where she lives. This was a big commitment but helped her decide this was definitely the work she wanted to do on a longer term basis.

Having followed all six Steps of The Career Navigation Cycle and being totally committed to her goals, Ruth is now well on the way to making her dream a reality. Whilst writing this book she has contacted me and has decided to take even more positive and inspired action. She has quit her job, is renting out her house and moving to Africa!!

Her story illustrates perfectly what happens when you take control of your life and your career, unlock your potential and become the architect of your own future! Her approach brilliantly encapsulates all the six Steps of the Cycle, as she has learnt to:

- **Let go and look forward** - break her past conditioning
- **Re-evaluate** – understand what is important to her in her career and life and WHY as her foundation to build from
- **Establish her true marketability** – who she is and what she has to offer the world and boost her confidence and self belief
- **Explore opportunities** – use volunteering to open up a whole new world for her
- **Decide what to do** – by piecing together the learning from Steps 2-4 and following her passion

- **Take positive action** – by setting her intent, being bold, taking personal responsibility, following through and being true to her values she has become the architect of her own future!

Navigate Your Way To A Brighter Future

Just as I achieved my breakthrough career change over a decade ago, so can you. The many inspirational examples I have shared with you in this book have also achieved their breakthroughs or are well on the way to doing so and illustrate without doubt that it is possible. My aim is to equip and inspire you to become the architect of your own future to win through redundancy and successfully relaunch **your** career, doing work you love.

Some final thoughts:

- Remember success is about the journey, so recognise your achievement in **completing** the Career Navigation Cycle process as a major step towards relaunching your career.
- Continue developing your networks, embracing Social Media and being opportunistic.
- Whatever you set out to do now is likely to evolve and change - you now have a toolkit to help achieve your vision of success now and for the future.
- The key to unlocking your potential is self awareness – continue to grow personally as well as professionally to become the best person you can be.
- Learn more and you will earn more!
- If you have found it difficult to make your transition on your own, seek expert help sooner rather than later, utilising the knowledge you gave gained from this book.

I have also provided many additional resources, including bonus extras not featured in the book, on my website. These tools are to help you work towards achieving your successful career change, regardless of whether this is as a result of redundancy or you are just stuck in a rut and unfulfilled in your current job. The toolkit contains:

- Free electronic worksheets for many of the key exercises in the book
- Free MP3 download -The first 30 minutes of my 'I Want A Career Change' 4CD/MP3 audio book set
- Free downloadable PDF with 5 pages of my Top Career Change Tips

You can download this toolkit of resources by registering at: **http://www.steveprestonthecareercatalyst.com**

I trust you have enjoyed your voyage of self discovery and I wish you well with your quest. Whatever your outcome, you will have learnt loads about yourself in the process. You have some excellent tools for life, should now understand the power of positive mindset, be less fearful of change and have my six Step Career Navigation Cycle to help you find fulfilment in your work and life. What could be better than this?

Regardless of how far you have come by reading this book, I would love to hear from you via my website **http://www.steveprestonthecareercatalyst.com** where you can sign up to receive my blog and newsletters. You can also place a review and 'like' on my Amazon book page: **http://amzn.to/ZUneWd**

If you have already become the architect of your own future and achieved your desired goal as a result of reading this book, many congratulations! It is great if you have now found a job or work that you love and achieve fulfilment to follow in the footsteps of the many inspiring examples in the book.

As you read this last page you will begin to truly understand the value of my Career Navigation Cycle and that **you can** win through redundancy and navigate your way to a brighter future. There is nothing to be gained by standing in the shadows, is there? *'Just Do It'* and have belief in yourself, as I have now given you the tools to pursue change and follow new opportunities. Just like me and the inspiring examples in this book, you will now appreciate the importance of taking that final Leap of Faith. If you follow through with the learning from this book, consider how it would feel to soar like an eagle and into a new era of your life? After you have read this final poem... just relax, close your eyes, visualise your journey so far and **you** now achieving a successful outcome!

'Come to the edge.'

'We can't. We're afraid.'

'Come to the edge.'

'We can't. We will fall!'

'Come to the edge.'

And they came.

And he pushed them.

And they flew.

Guillaume Apollinaire,
Poet, Playwright and Novelist, 1880-1918

USEFUL & INSPIRING RESOURCES

Navigate Your Way To A Brighter Future

Steve has created a toolkit of additional resources for you, including many **bonus extras** not featured in the book. These tools are to help you work towards achieving a successful career change, regardless of whether this is as a result of redundancy or you are just stuck in a rut and unfulfilled in your current job. **The toolkit contains:**

- Free electronic worksheets for many of the key exercises in the book
- Free MP3 download -The first 30 minutes of Steve's highly acclaimed 'I Want A Career Change' 4CD/MP3 audio book set
- Free downloadable PDF with 5 pages of Top Career Change Tips to help your career change quest, including a link to Steve's special online Career Values and Needs Tool - **use code CVN10 to save £10!**

You can download this toolkit of resources by registering at:
http://www.steveprestonthecareercatalyst.com

In addition, the following is Steve's suggested list of reading, audio books, DVDs, websites and web links to support your journey in Navigating your way to a brighter future:

Business Networking
Gibson, Gail - *Making Connections – How to network effectively to build better business relationships*

Business Start up
Bridger, Steve - *Success Before Start Up*
http://www.startuptosuccess.co.uk

Career Advice blog
Available at:
http://www.smpcareeradvice.com

Career Change
Preston, Steve - *I Want A Career Change, Online Career Change & Transition Programme*

SPECIAL READER OFFER:
Save £100 using code WTR100 in Coupon box

Available at:
http://www.steveprestonthecareercatalyst.com/index.php/i-want-a-career-change/online-programme

Preston, Steve - *I Want A Career Change – 6 steps to navigate the way to a brighter future*, Audio book CD / MP3 set, available at:
http://www.steveprestonthecareercatalyst.com/index.php/i-want-a-career-change

Preston, Steve – *I Want A Career Change - Breakthrough Career Change & Transition Masterclass*, available at: **http://www.steveprestonthecareercatalyst.com/index.php/masterclasses/17-breakthrough-career-change-transition-masterclass**

Career Coaching
Steve Preston The Career Catalyst, available at:
http://www.steveprestonthecareercatalyst.com/index.php/coaching

Career & Personal Development
Steve Preston The Career Catalyst, available at:
http://www.steveprestonthecareercatalyst.com

SMP Solutions (Career & People Development) Ltd, available at:
http://www.smp-solutions.co.uk

Career Values & Needs Tool
Steve Preston The Career Catalyst

SPECIAL READER OFFER:
Save £10 using code CVN10 in Coupon box

Available at:
http://www.steveprestonthecareercatalyst.com/index.php/component/hikashop/product/cid-33?Itemid=121

CV's
Lees, John - *Knockout CV*

SMP Solutions (Career & People Development) Ltd, *Creating a Successful CV*, available at:
http://www.smp-solutions.co.uk/PersonalCareerPersonalDevelopment/SuccessfulCVWriting.aspx

Emotional Intelligence
Available at:
http://danielgoleman.info
http://www.rochemartin.co.uk

Hidden Job Market
Perkins, Graham - *CV's and Hidden Approaches*

Interview Skills
Lees, John – *Top Answers to Tough Questions*

SMP Solutions (Career & People Development) Ltd, Interview Skills, available at:
http://www.smp-solutions.co.uk/Personal/CareerPersonalDevelopment/InterviewSkills.aspx

Mind Mapping tools
Available at:
http://www.xmind.net

Outplacement and Career Transition support
(for companies making redundancies)
SMP Solutions (Career & People Development) Ltd, Outplacement, available at:
http://www.smp-solutions.co.uk/business/RedundancyOutplacementandCareerManagement.aspx

Personal Branding
Smith, Debbie - *Imagine Your Potential*
Available at:
http://www.imagineyourpotential.co.uk

Purkiss, John & Royston - Lee, David - *Brand You – Turn Your Unique Talents into a Winning Formula*

Portfolio Careers & Lifestyle

Preston, Steve & Gibson, Gail - *How Colourful is Your Umbrella – Creating Your Portfolio of Choice,* Portfolio Career & Lifestyle Masterclasses, Steve Preston The Career Catalyst, available at:
http://www.steveprestonthecareercatalyst.com/index.php/masterclasses/14-how-colourful-is-your-umbrella

Preston, Steve & Gibson, Gail - *How Colourful is Your Umbrella? - Create a working life where you'll enjoy Mondays as much as Fridays!* Audio CD and MP3 set, available at:
http://www.steveprestonthecareercatalyst.com/index.php/component/hikashop/product/cid-44?Itemid=121

Hopson, Barrie & Ledger, Katie - *And What Do You Do? – 10 Steps To Creating A Portfolio Career*

Personal Development

Agness, Lesley - *Change Your Life with NLP – The Powerful way to make your whole life better*

Byrne, Rhonda - *The Secret*

Covey, Stephen - *The 7 Habits of Highly Effective People*

Berman-Fortang, Laura - *Living Your Best Life*

Godin, Seth - *Purple Cow: Transform Your Business By Being Remarkable*

Godin, Seth - *The Dip: The Extraordinary benefits of knowing when to quit (and when to stick)*

Godin, Seth – *The Icarus Deception – how high will you fly?*

Handy, Charles – *The Age of Unreason*

Hicks, Esther & Hicks, Jerry *The Law of Attraction - How to Make it Work for You*

Johnson, Spencer – *Who Moved My Cheese – An Amazing Way to Deal With Change In Your Work and In Your Life*

Rohn, Jim – *Building Your Network Marketing Business*

Rohn, Jim – *12 Pillars of Success*

Sammarco, Leda - *Finding the Gold: One girl's search for her purpose in life*

Tracy, Brian – *The New Psychology of Achievement*

Tracy, Brian – *The Universal Laws of Success & Achievement*

Vitale, Joe – *The Missing Secret*

Williams, Nick – *The Business You Were Born To Create*

Williams, Roy- *Free the Beagle- A Journey to Destinae*

Ziglar, Zig – *How to Stay Motivated – Changing the Picture*

Vision Boards
Available at:
http://www.visionboardsite.com

Visualization
Pulos, Lee - *The Power of Visualization*

ABOUT

Steve Preston

Recognised as 'The Career Catalyst', Steve has transformed the lives and careers of thousands of people at all levels and at different stages of their careers, across many business sectors. An accredited, expert career coach he is passionate about helping people unlock their potential and thrives on sharing his knowledge and experience to inspire people to follow their passions.

In addition to his breakthrough coaching, innovative online programmes and audio books, he runs unique Masterclasses to help people work through options for a career change and also to develop a portfolio career and a different working lifestyle. His company SMP Solutions (Career & People Development) Ltd also provides quality outplacement programmes for organisations laying off staff. Steve has written numerous articles for his blogs, trade journals, career and personal development websites in the UK and US and is an established speaker and keynote at high profile career events, conferences and professional associations.

How to book or connect with Steve

If you would like to invite Steve to speak at your event, engage him to coach or mentor you, sign up for his blogs, learn more about his many products and services or just become part of his online communities, please contact him by any of the following means…

Office tel: **01895 474 887**

Email: **steve@steveprestonthecareercatalyst.com**

Steve Preston The Career Catalyst website:
http://www.steveprestonthecareercatalyst.com

Steve Preston The Career Catalyst blog:
http://www.steveprestonthecareercatalyst.com/index.php/blog

Facebook:
http://www.facebook.com/TheCareerCatalyst

Twitter:
https://twitter.com/stevempreston
https://twitter.com/smpsolutions

LinkedIn:
http://www.linkedin.com/in/steveprestonsmpsolutions

SMP Career Advice Blog:
http://www.smpcareeradvice.com

SMP Solutions *(Career & People Development)* **Ltd:**
www.smp-solutions.co.uk

YouTube Channels:
http://www.youtube.com/channel/UCj0dyVi9gborbV0fLSZ7iow/videos?view=0
http://www.youtube.com/user/smpsolutions

ABOUT

Tara Winona

Art and words woven together, capturing the power of life changing moments...

Tara Winona creates images with the desire to tell stories. Often with double meanings, Tara's art seeks to celebrate the power of the imagination and capture the magic of life changing moments, motivated by an innate desire to see us all reach our potential. Her inspiration comes from her life adventures, a love of storytelling and an endless fascination with nature.

Originally, Tara trained as a designer and illustrator in Australia... then for many years, she created and directed spectaculars internationally, painting with lasers, lights, fireworks and sound. She made homes in Milan, Paris and London, travelled the world several times, became two languages wiser and able to say 'thank you' in at least 30. She has had a lot of crazy adventures, some of them particularly hair raising, which she might write a book about one of these days...

One day, Tara took a leap of faith and rented an art studio. She began to create just for herself. A wonderful fulfilling love affair was rekindled and thus Tara began to 'follow her star'.

Steve and Tara met when she was showing her 'Reach for Your Dreams' paintings - a series which show a little red headed girl taking leaps of faith and learning to be courageous. Steve 'got it' and an instant friendship was formed. They talked about Steve writing a book and Tara doing the illustrations and, one day, Steve took his own leap of faith. As Steve says, *"life is too short to not do what you love!"*

Now an artist, illustrator, writer and creative director, Tara Winona works from her studio nestled along the canal banks of Johnsons Island in London, absentmindedly dipping paint brushes in her tea as the kingfishers flash past. And eating chocolate.

www.tarawinona.com